TIGER!

TIGER!

TIGER!

VOLUME ONE

A COLLECTION OF SCATTERED THOUGHTS AND MOMENTS THAT SOMEHOW EQUAL A WHOLE

RED
WINDOW

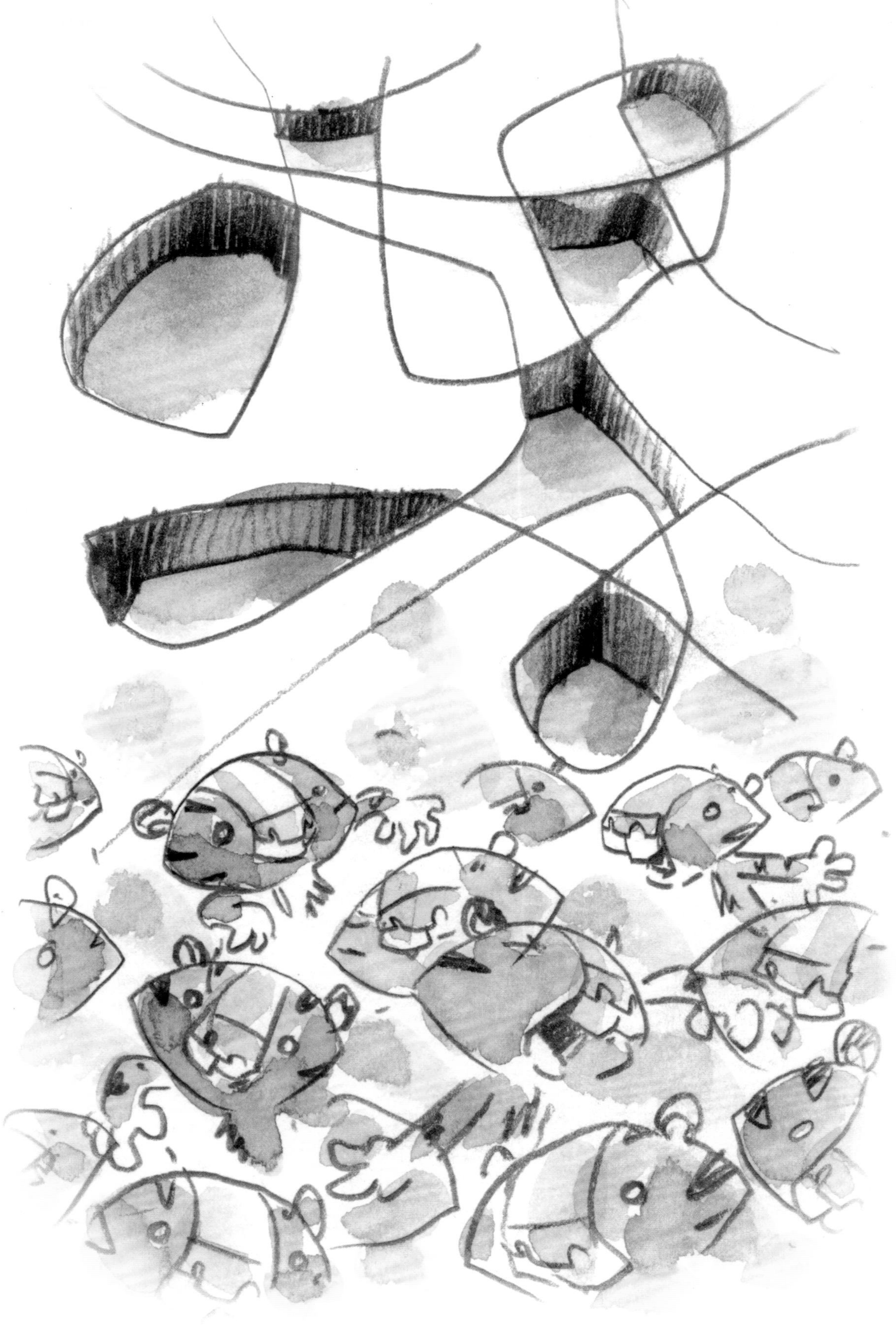

Tiger!Tiger!Tiger! Published by Red Window, Inc., P.O. Box 99408, Emeryville, California 94608-9408, www.scottmorse.com
3219 8371

isbn 978-0-9774715-3-9 | 10 9 8 7 6 5 4 3 2 1

Distributed by AdHouse Books | www.AdHouseBooks.com
First Printing, 2008. Printed in China.

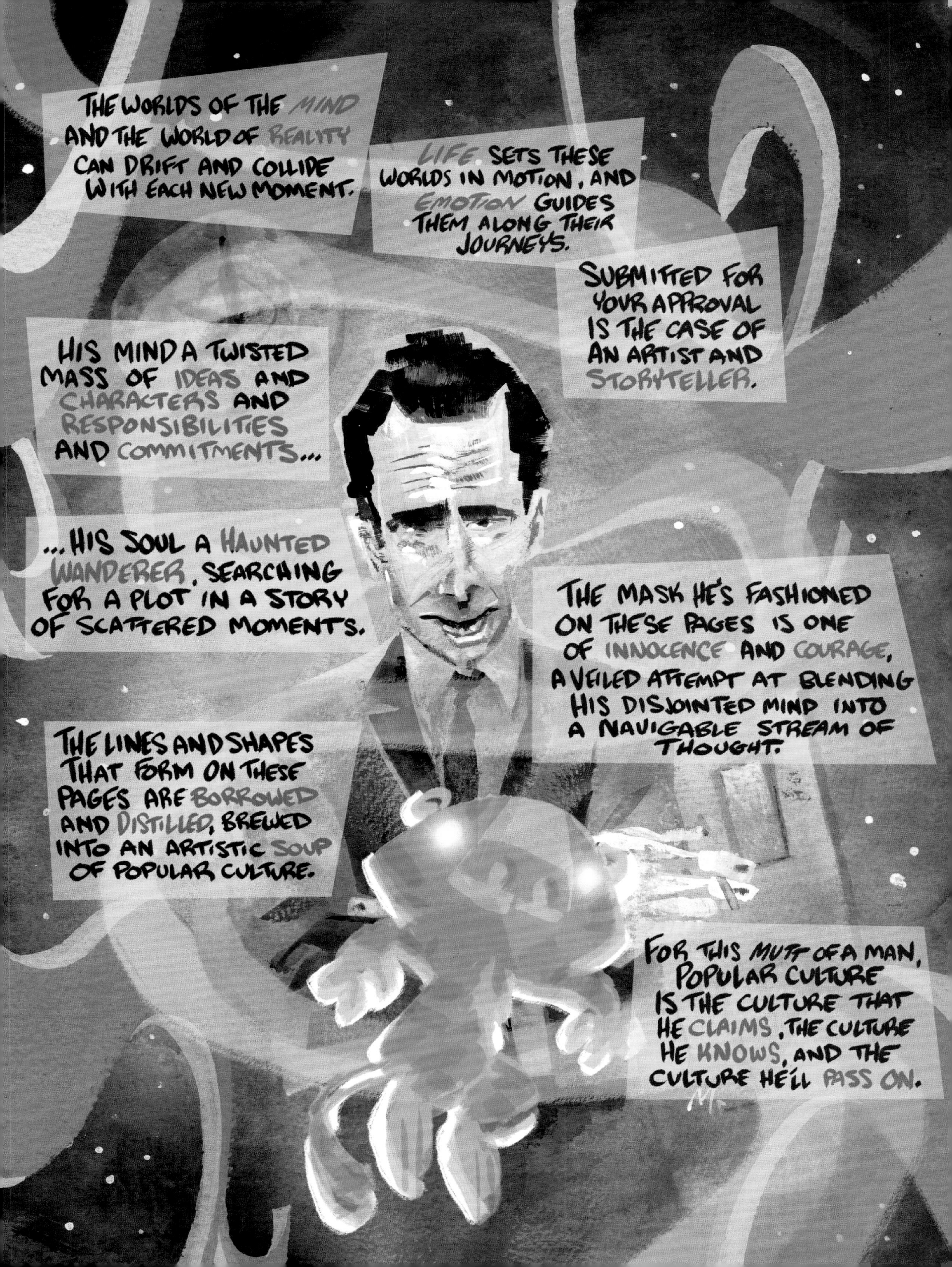
THE WORLDS OF THE MIND AND THE WORLD OF REALITY CAN DRIFT AND COLLIDE WITH EACH NEW MOMENT.
LIFE SETS THESE WORLDS IN MOTION, AND EMOTION GUIDES THEM ALONG THEIR JOURNEYS.
SUBMITTED FOR YOUR APPROVAL IS THE CASE OF AN ARTIST AND STORYTELLER.
HIS MIND A TWISTED MASS OF IDEAS AND CHARACTERS AND RESPONSIBILITIES AND COMMITMENTS...
...HIS SOUL A HAUNTED WANDERER, SEARCHING FOR A PLOT IN A STORY OF SCATTERED MOMENTS.
THE MASK HE'S FASHIONED ON THESE PAGES IS ONE OF INNOCENCE AND COURAGE, A VEILED ATTEMPT AT BLENDING HIS DISJOINTED MIND INTO A NAVIGABLE STREAM OF THOUGHT.
THE LINES AND SHAPES THAT FORM ON THESE PAGES ARE BORROWED AND DISTILLED, BREWED INTO AN ARTISTIC SOUP OF POPULAR CULTURE.
FOR THIS MUTT OF A MAN, POPULAR CULTURE IS THE CULTURE THAT HE CLAIMS, THE CULTURE HE KNOWS, AND THE CULTURE HE'LL PASS ON.

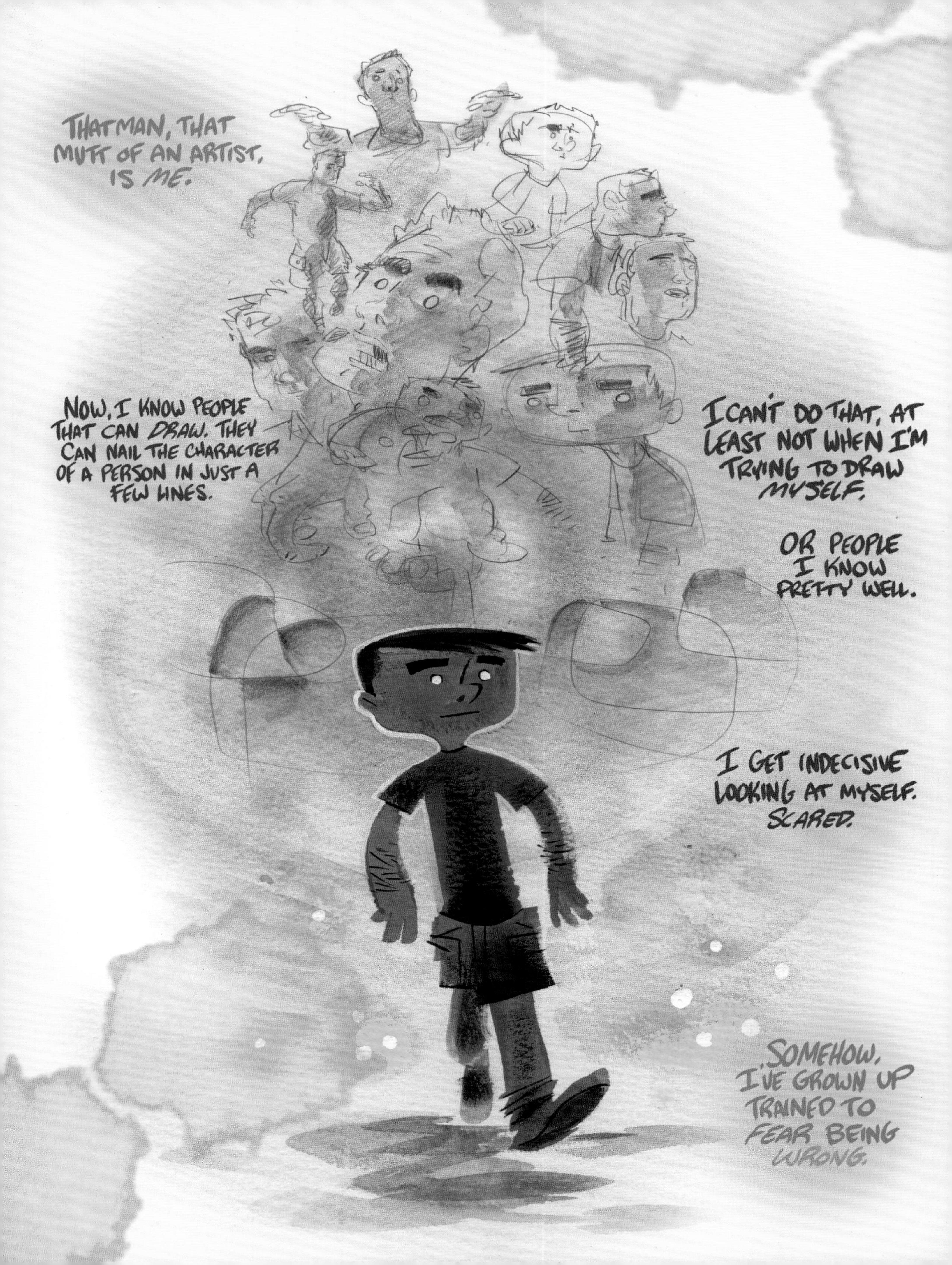
THATMAN, THAT MUTT OF AN ARTIST, IS *ME*.
NOW, I KNOW PEOPLE THAT CAN *DRAW*. THEY CAN NAIL THE CHARACTER OF A PERSON IN JUST A FEW LINES.
I CAN'T DO THAT, AT LEAST NOT WHEN I'M TRYING TO DRAW *MYSELF*.
OR PEOPLE I KNOW PRETTY WELL.
I GET INDECISIVE LOOKING AT MYSELF. *SCARED*.
SOMEHOW, I'VE GROWN UP TRAINED TO *FEAR BEING WRONG*.

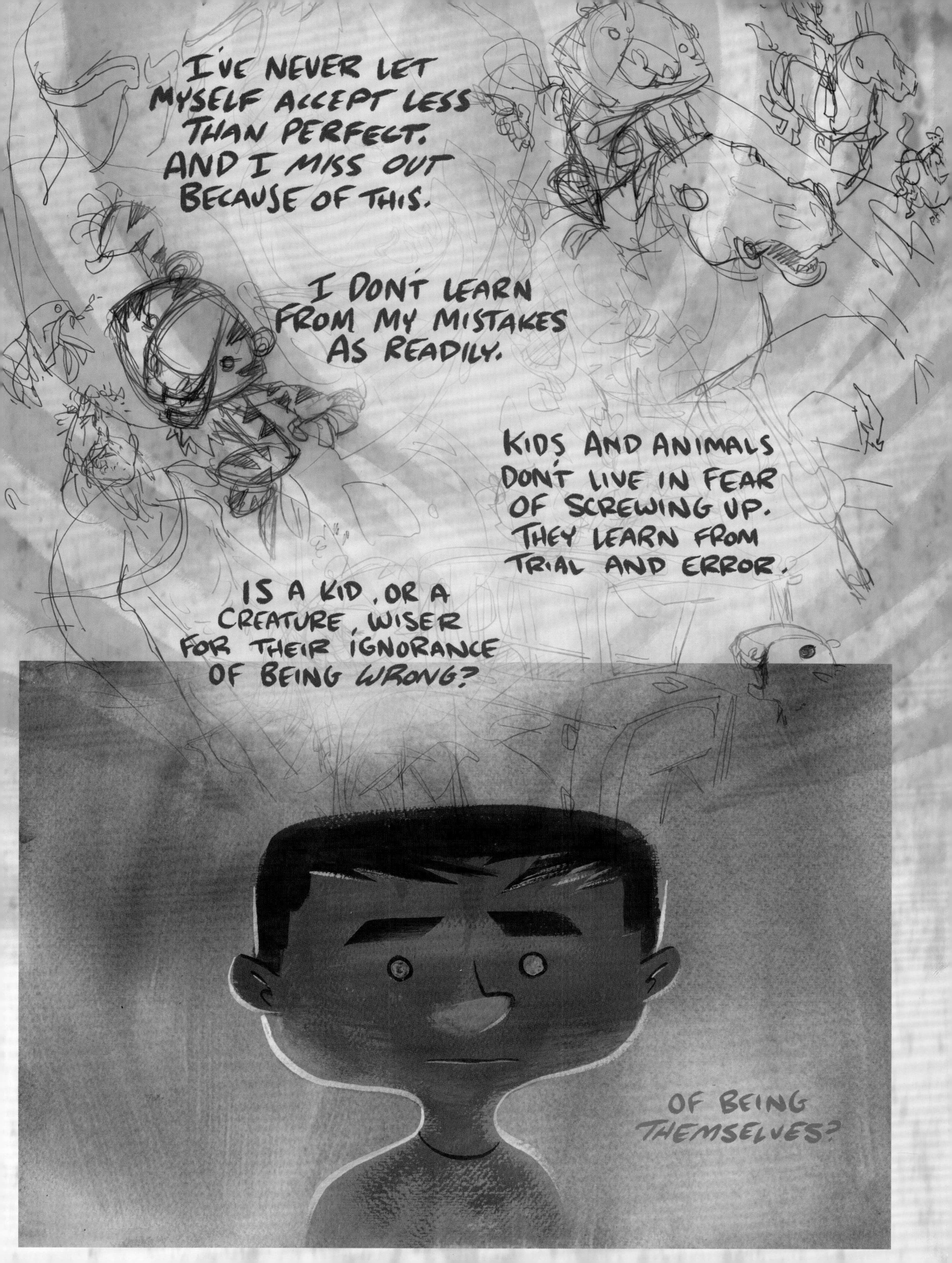
I'VE NEVER LET MYSELF ACCEPT LESS THAN PERFECT. AND I MISS OUT BECAUSE OF THIS.
I DON'T LEARN FROM MY MISTAKES AS READILY.
KIDS AND ANIMALS DON'T LIVE IN FEAR OF SCREWING UP. THEY LEARN FROM TRIAL AND ERROR.
IS A KID, OR A CREATURE, WISER FOR THEIR IGNORANCE OF BEING WRONG?
OF BEING THEMSELVES?

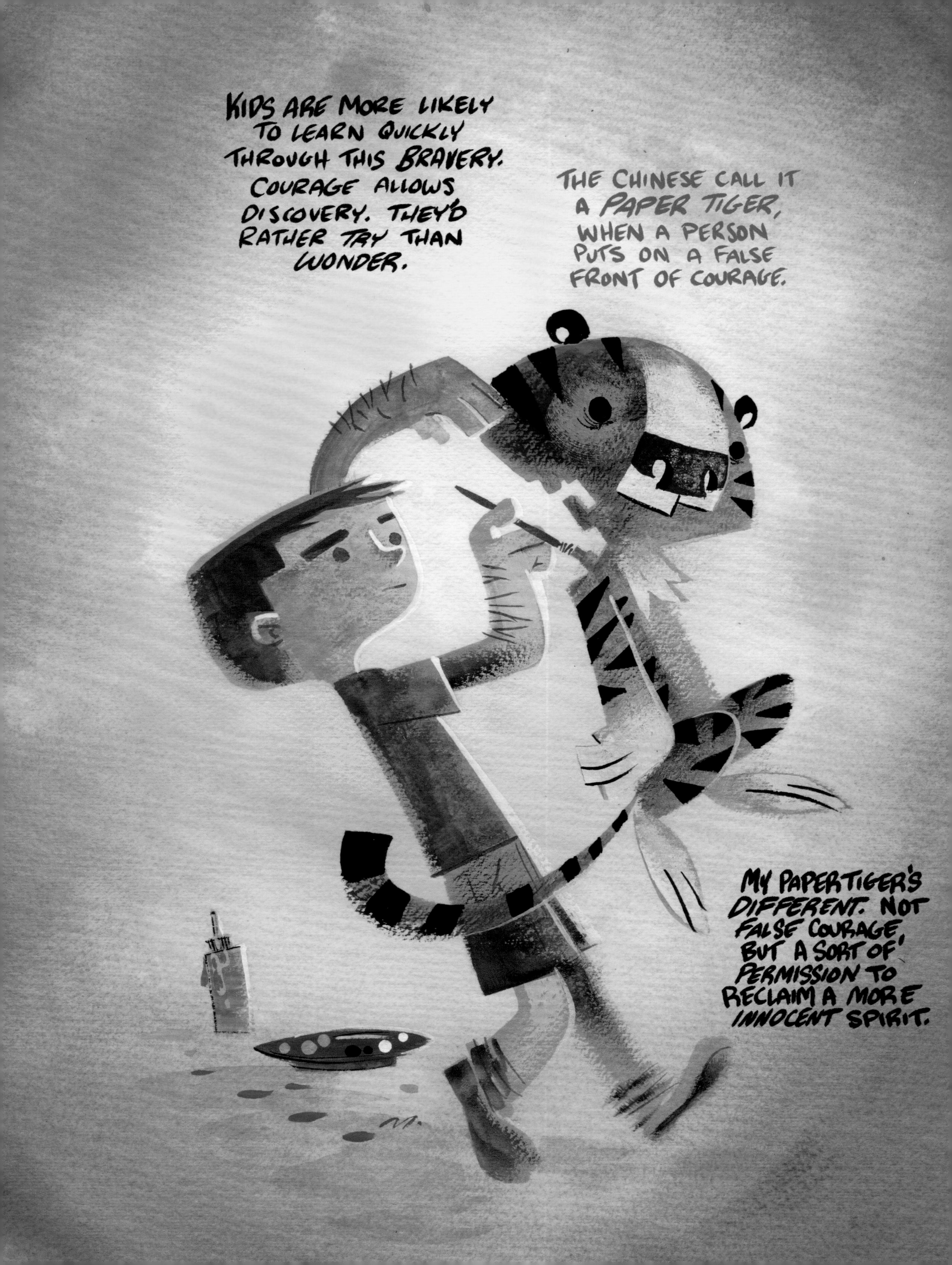
KIDS ARE MORE LIKELY TO LEARN QUICKLY THROUGH THIS BRAVERY. COURAGE ALLOWS DISCOVERY. THEY'D RATHER TRY THAN WONDER.
THE CHINESE CALL IT A PAPER TIGER, WHEN A PERSON PUTS ON A FALSE FRONT OF COURAGE.
MY PAPERTIGER'S DIFFERENT. NOT FALSE COURAGE, BUT A SORT OF PERMISSION TO RECLAIM A MORE INNOCENT SPIRIT.

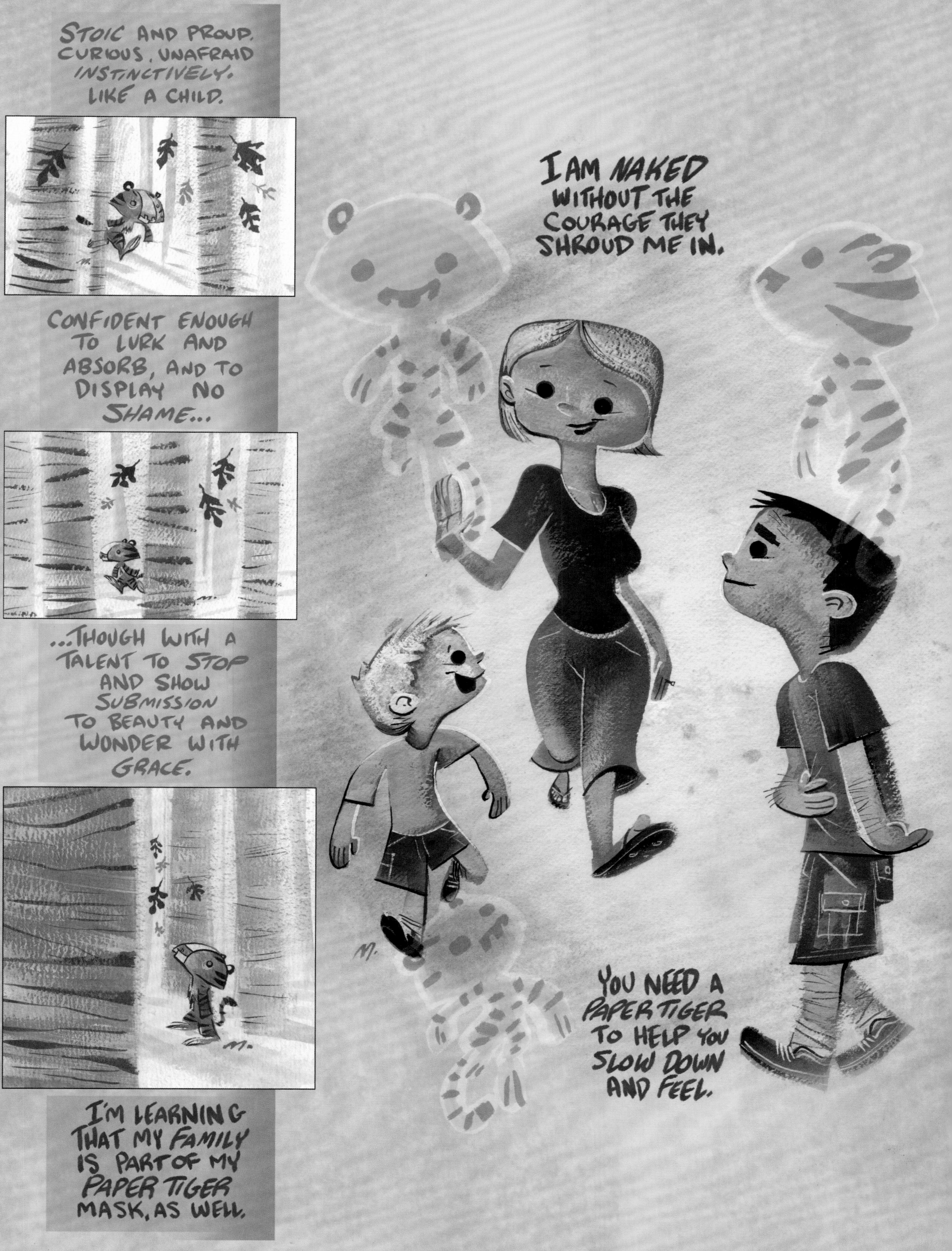
STOIC AND PROUD, CURIOUS, UNAFRAID INSTINCTIVELY. LIKE A CHILD.
CONFIDENT ENOUGH TO LURK AND ABSORB, AND TO DISPLAY NO SHAME...
...THOUGH WITH A TALENT TO STOP AND SHOW SUBMISSION TO BEAUTY AND WONDER WITH GRACE.
I'M LEARNING THAT MY FAMILY IS PART OF MY PAPER TIGER MASK, AS WELL.
I AM NAKED WITHOUT THE COURAGE THEY SHROUD ME IN.
YOU NEED A PAPER TIGER TO HELP YOU SLOW DOWN AND FEEL.

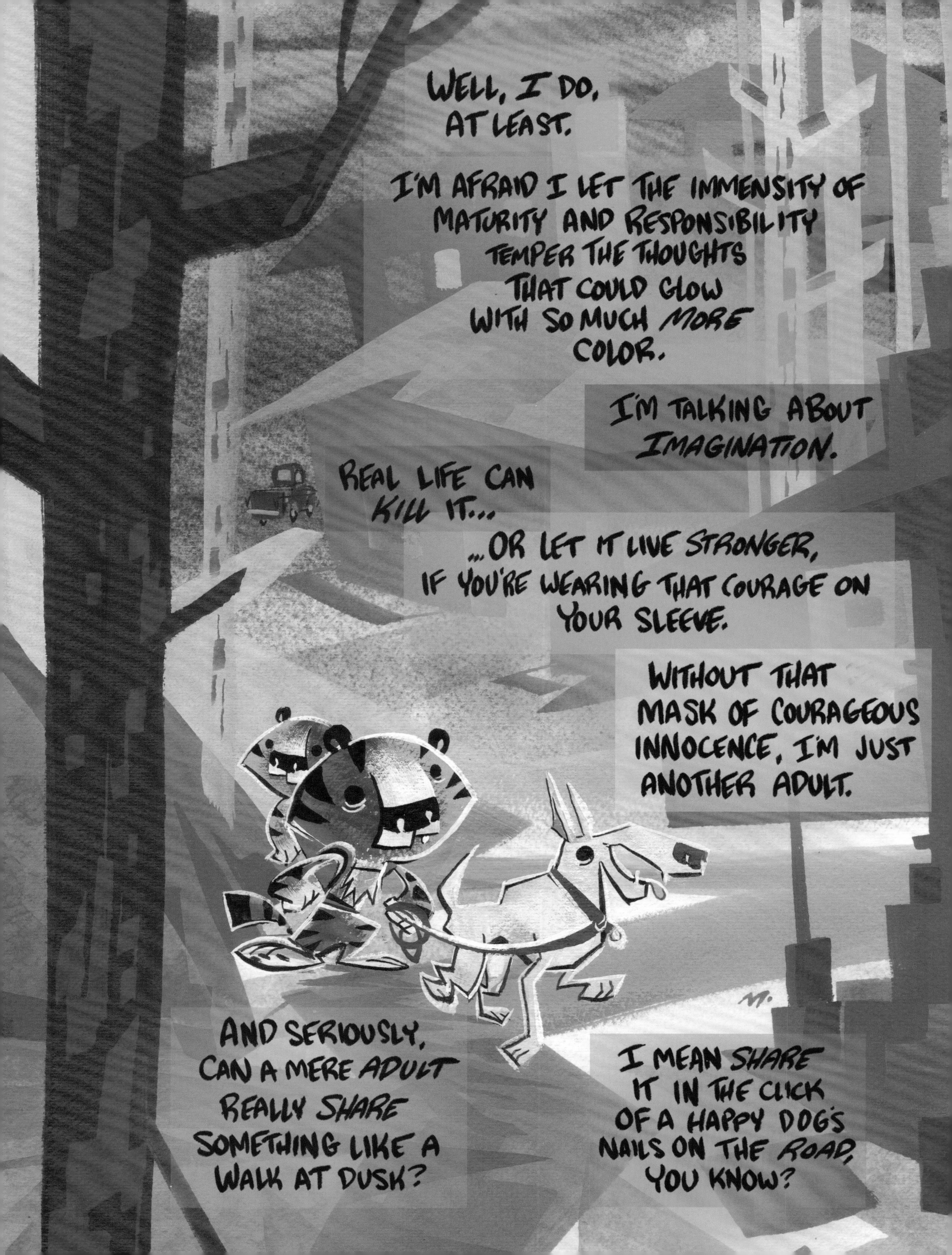
WELL, I DO, AT LEAST.
I'M AFRAID I LET THE IMMENSITY OF MATURITY AND RESPONSIBILITY TEMPER THE THOUGHTS THAT COULD GLOW WITH SO MUCH *MORE* COLOR.
I'M TALKING ABOUT *IMAGINATION*.
REAL LIFE CAN *KILL* IT...
...OR LET IT LIVE *STRONGER*, IF YOU'RE WEARING THAT COURAGE ON YOUR SLEEVE.
WITHOUT THAT MASK OF COURAGEOUS INNOCENCE, I'M JUST ANOTHER ADULT.
AND SERIOUSLY, CAN A MERE *ADULT* REALLY *SHARE* SOMETHING LIKE A WALK AT DUSK?
I MEAN *SHARE* IT IN THE CLICK OF A HAPPY DOG'S NAILS ON THE *ROAD*, YOU KNOW?

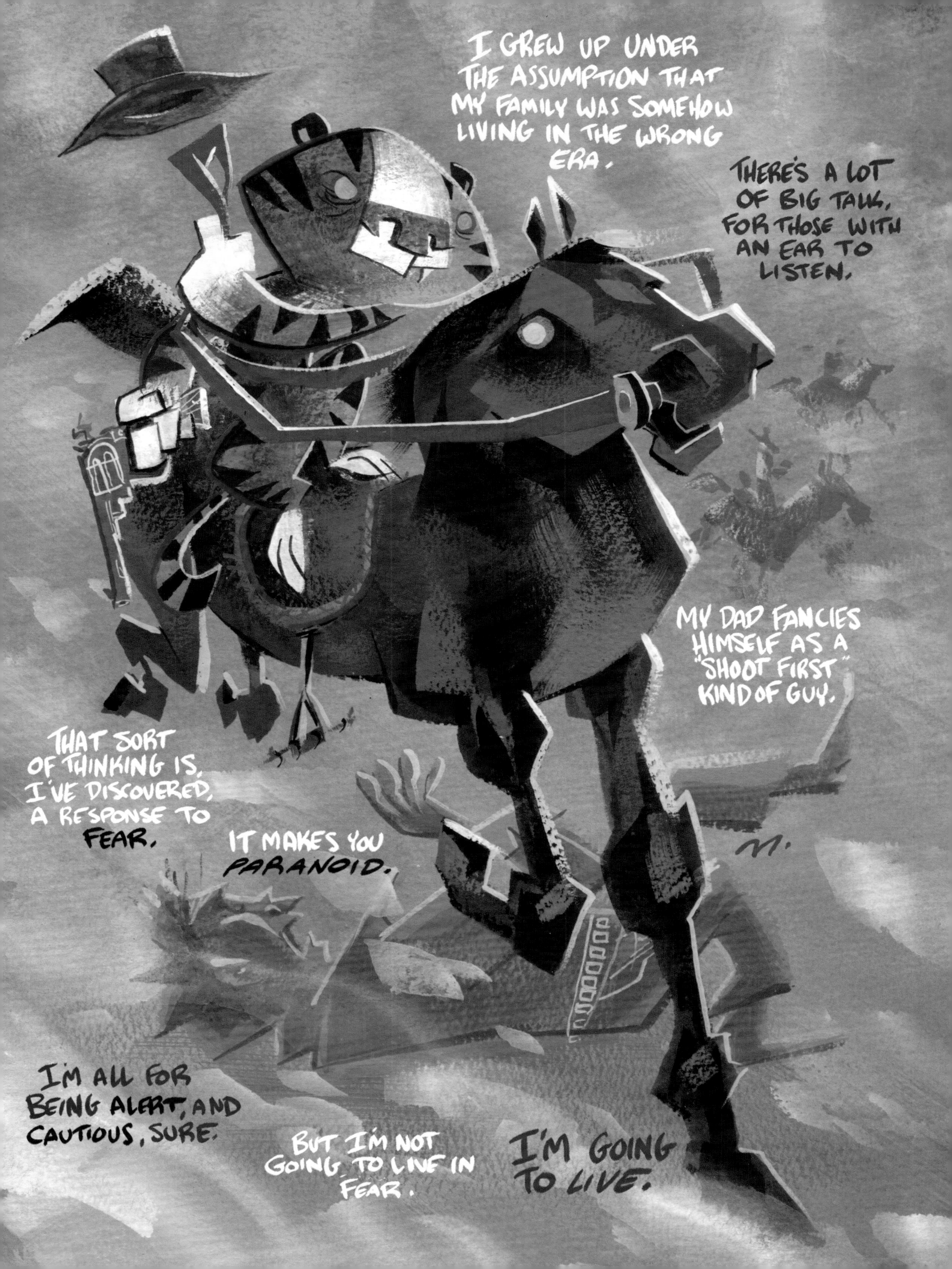

I GREW UP UNDER THE ASSUMPTION THAT MY FAMILY WAS SOMEHOW LIVING IN THE WRONG ERA.
THERE'S A LOT OF BIG TALK, FOR THOSE WITH AN EAR TO LISTEN.
MY DAD FANCIES HIMSELF AS A "SHOOT FIRST" KIND OF GUY.
THAT SORT OF THINKING IS, I'VE DISCOVERED, A RESPONSE TO FEAR.
IT MAKES YOU PARANOID.
I'M ALL FOR BEING ALERT, AND CAUTIOUS, SURE.
BUT I'M NOT GOING TO LIVE IN FEAR.
I'M GOING TO LIVE.

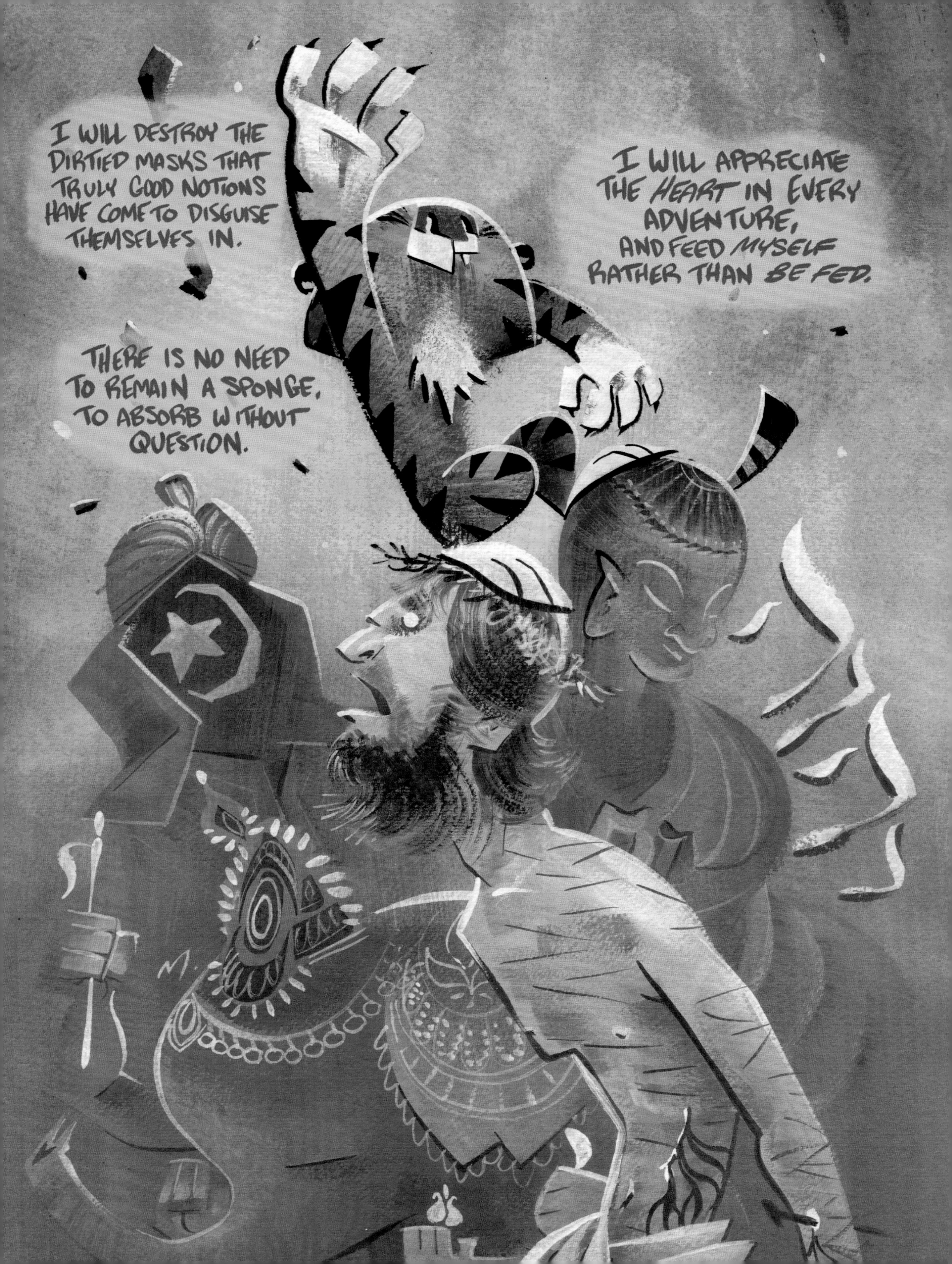
I WILL DESTROY THE DIRTIED MASKS THAT TRULY GOOD NOTIONS HAVE COME TO DISGUISE THEMSELVES IN.
I WILL APPRECIATE THE *HEART* IN EVERY ADVENTURE, AND FEED *MYSELF* RATHER THAN *BE FED.*
THERE IS NO NEED TO REMAIN A SPONGE, TO ABSORB WITHOUT QUESTION.

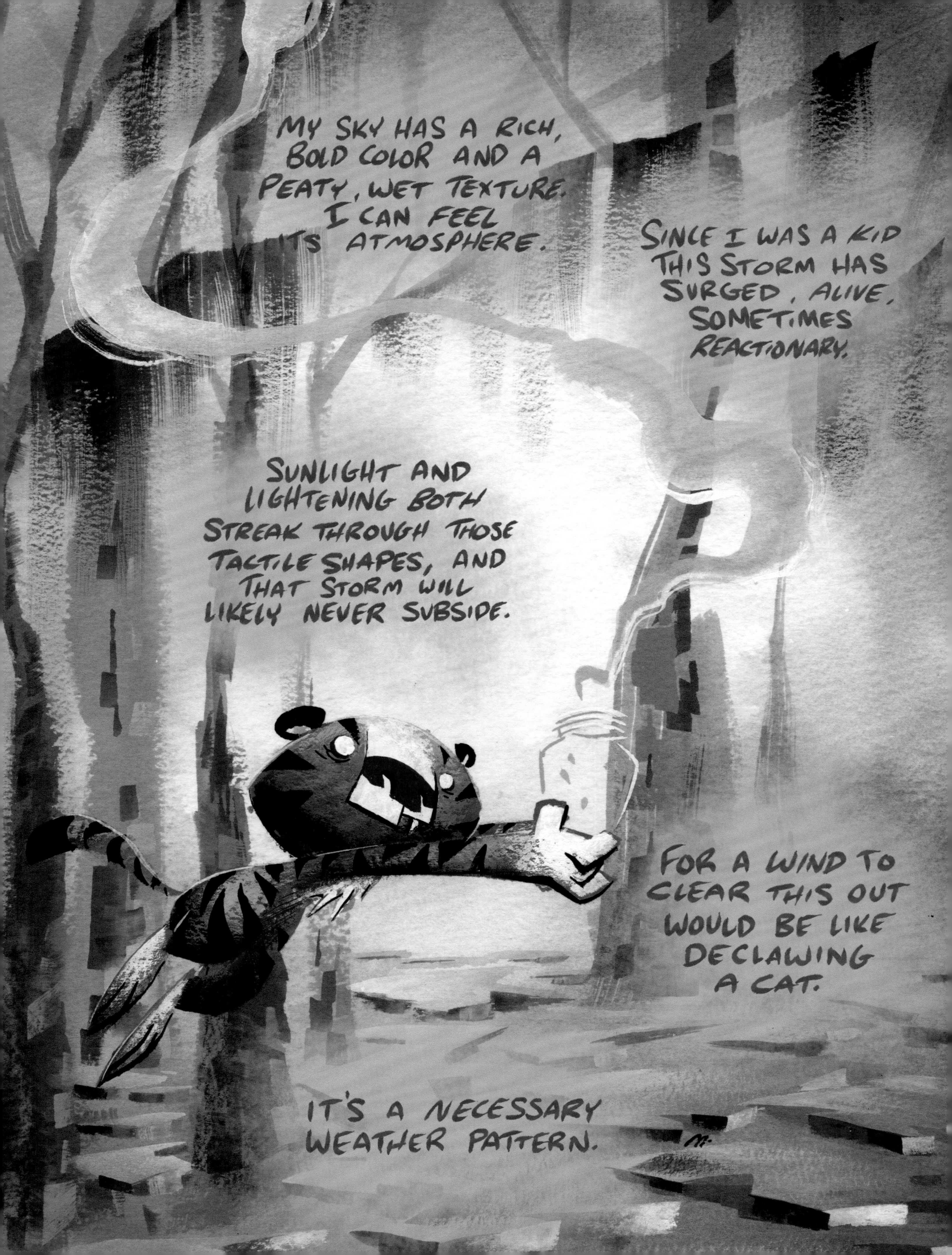
MY SKY HAS A RICH, BOLD COLOR AND A PEATY, WET TEXTURE. I CAN FEEL ITS ATMOSPHERE.
SINCE I WAS A KID THIS STORM HAS SURGED, ALIVE, SOMETIMES REACTIONARY.
SUNLIGHT AND LIGHTENING BOTH STREAK THROUGH THOSE TACTILE SHAPES, AND THAT STORM WILL LIKELY NEVER SUBSIDE.
FOR A WIND TO CLEAR THIS OUT WOULD BE LIKE DECLAWING A CAT.
IT'S A NECESSARY WEATHER PATTERN.

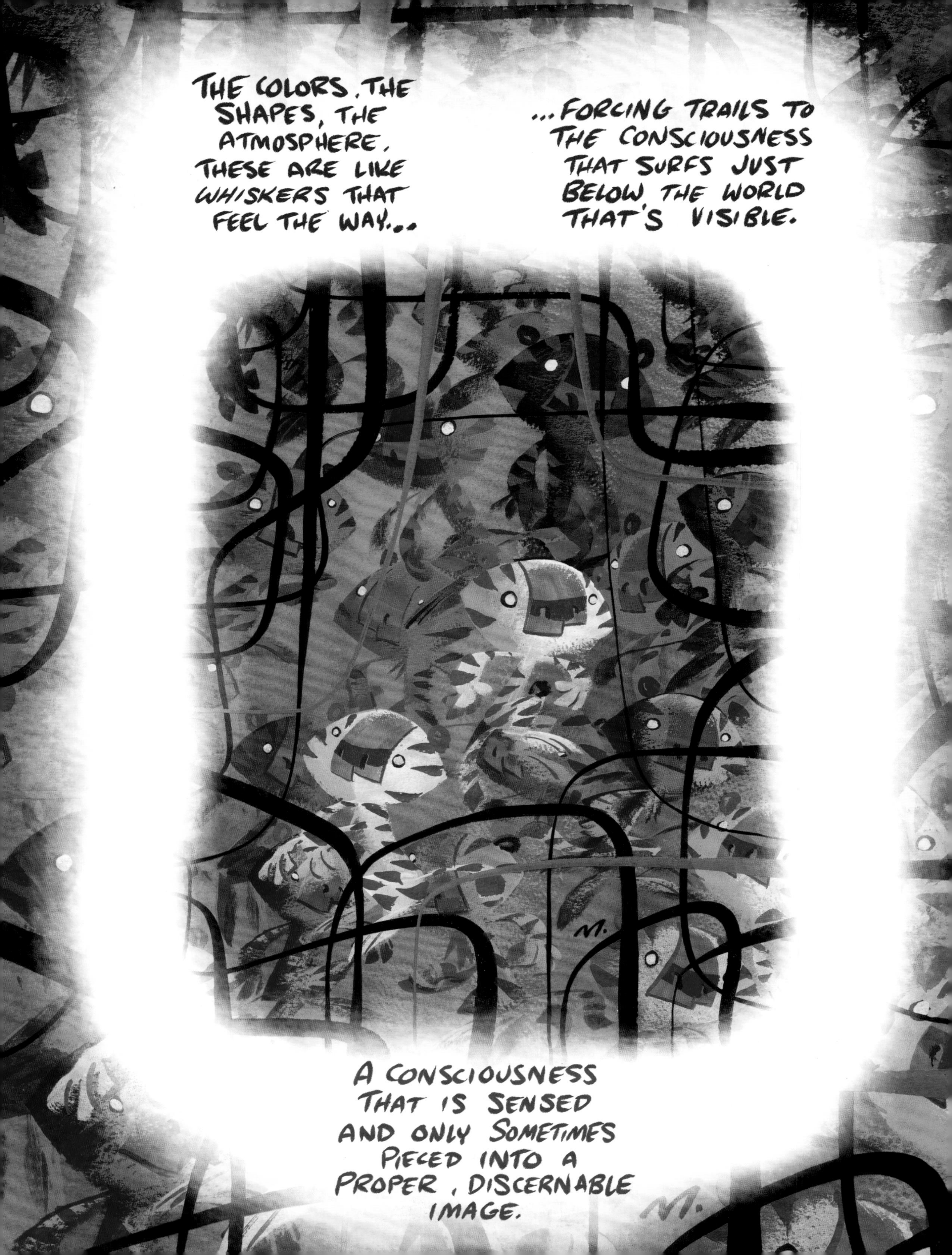
THE COLORS, THE SHAPES, THE ATMOSPHERE. THESE ARE LIKE WHISKERS THAT FEEL THE WAY...
...FORCING TRAILS TO THE CONSCIOUSNESS THAT SURFS JUST BELOW THE WORLD THAT'S VISIBLE.
A CONSCIOUSNESS THAT IS SENSED AND ONLY SOMETIMES PIECED INTO A PROPER, DISCERNABLE IMAGE.

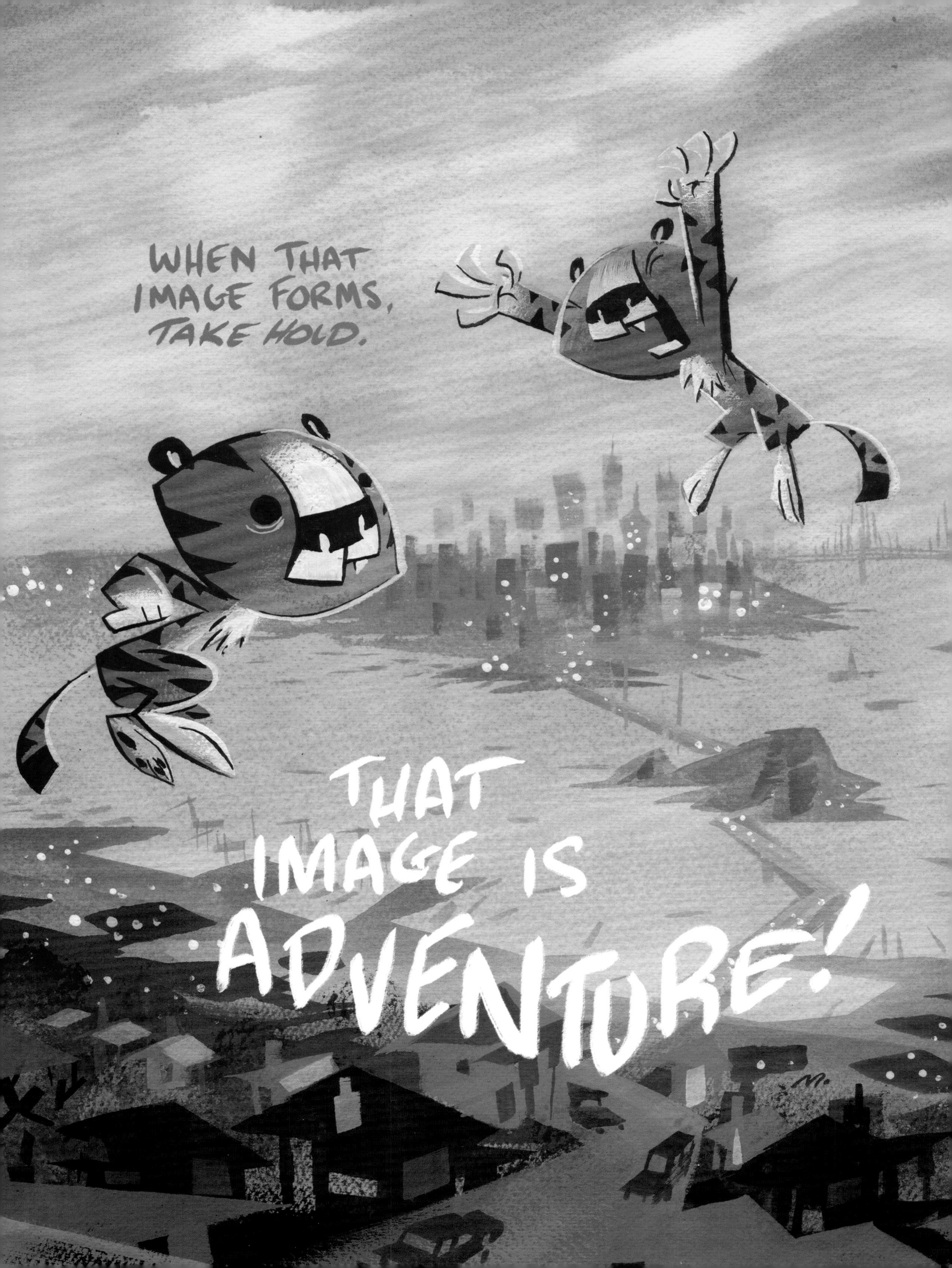
WHEN THAT IMAGE FORMS, TAKE HOLD.
THAT IMAGE IS ADVENTURE!

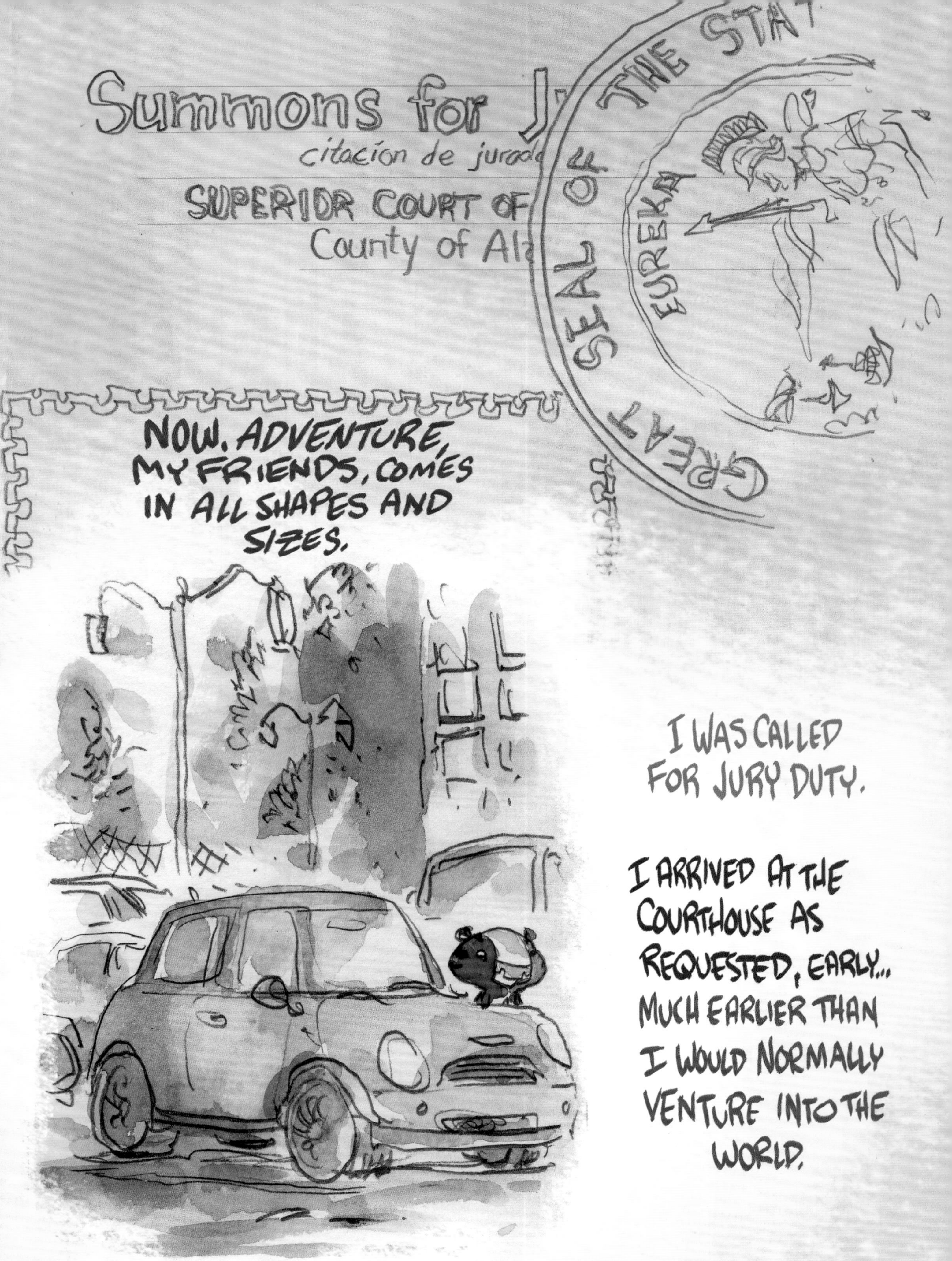
Summons for J
citación de jurad
SUPERIOR COURT OF
County of Al
GREAT SEAL OF THE STAT
EUREKA
NOW, ADVENTURE, MY FRIENDS, COMES IN ALL SHAPES AND SIZES.
I WAS CALLED FOR JURY DUTY.
I ARRIVED AT THE COURTHOUSE AS REQUESTED, EARLY... MUCH EARLIER THAN I WOULD NORMALLY VENTURE INTO THE WORLD.

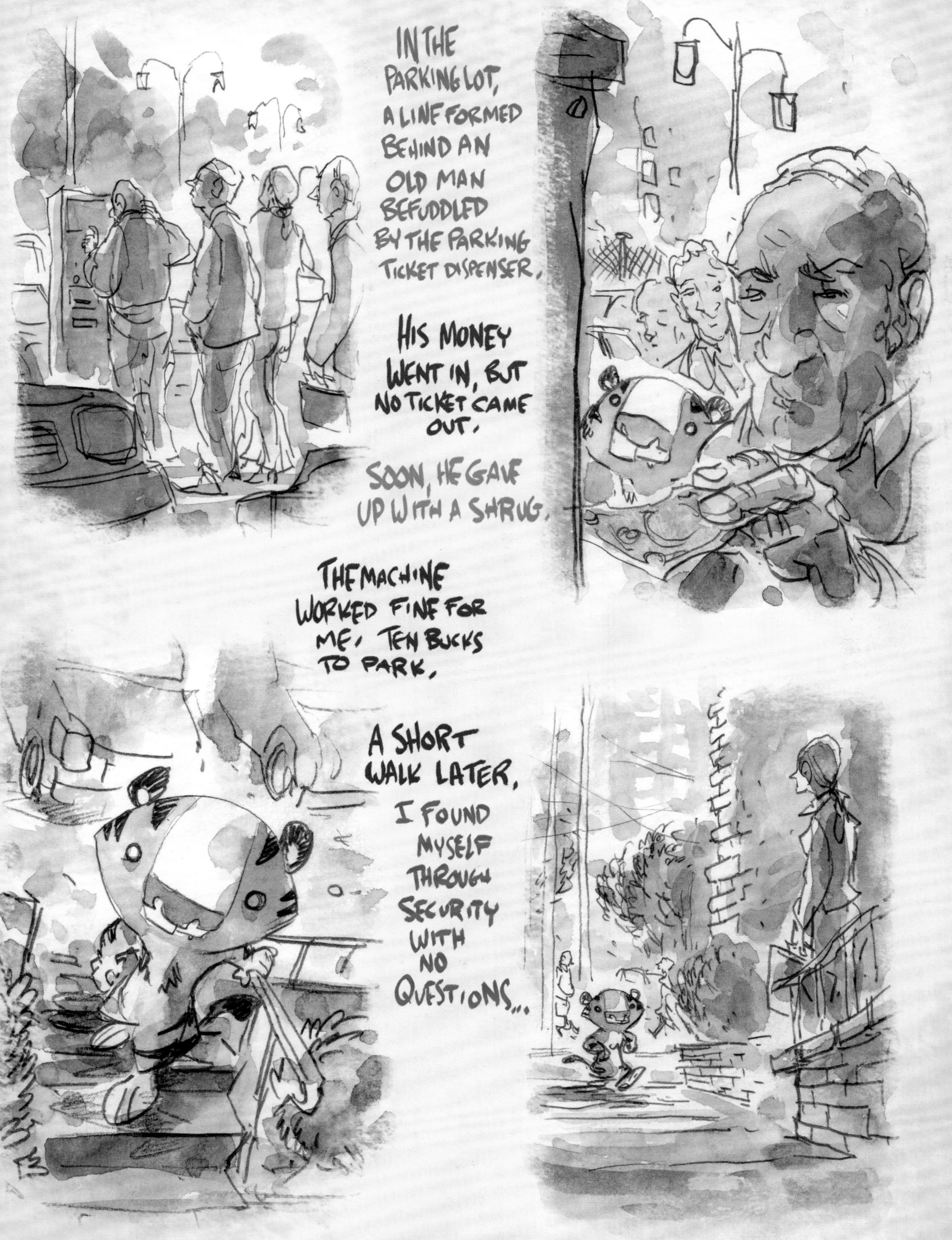
IN THE PARKING LOT, A LINE FORMED BEHIND AN OLD MAN BEFUDDLED BY THE PARKING TICKET DISPENSER.
HIS MONEY WENT IN, BUT NO TICKET CAME OUT.
SOON, HE GAVE UP WITH A SHRUG.
THE MACHINE WORKED FINE FOR ME. TEN BUCKS TO PARK.
A SHORT WALK LATER, I FOUND MYSELF THROUGH SECURITY WITH NO QUESTIONS...

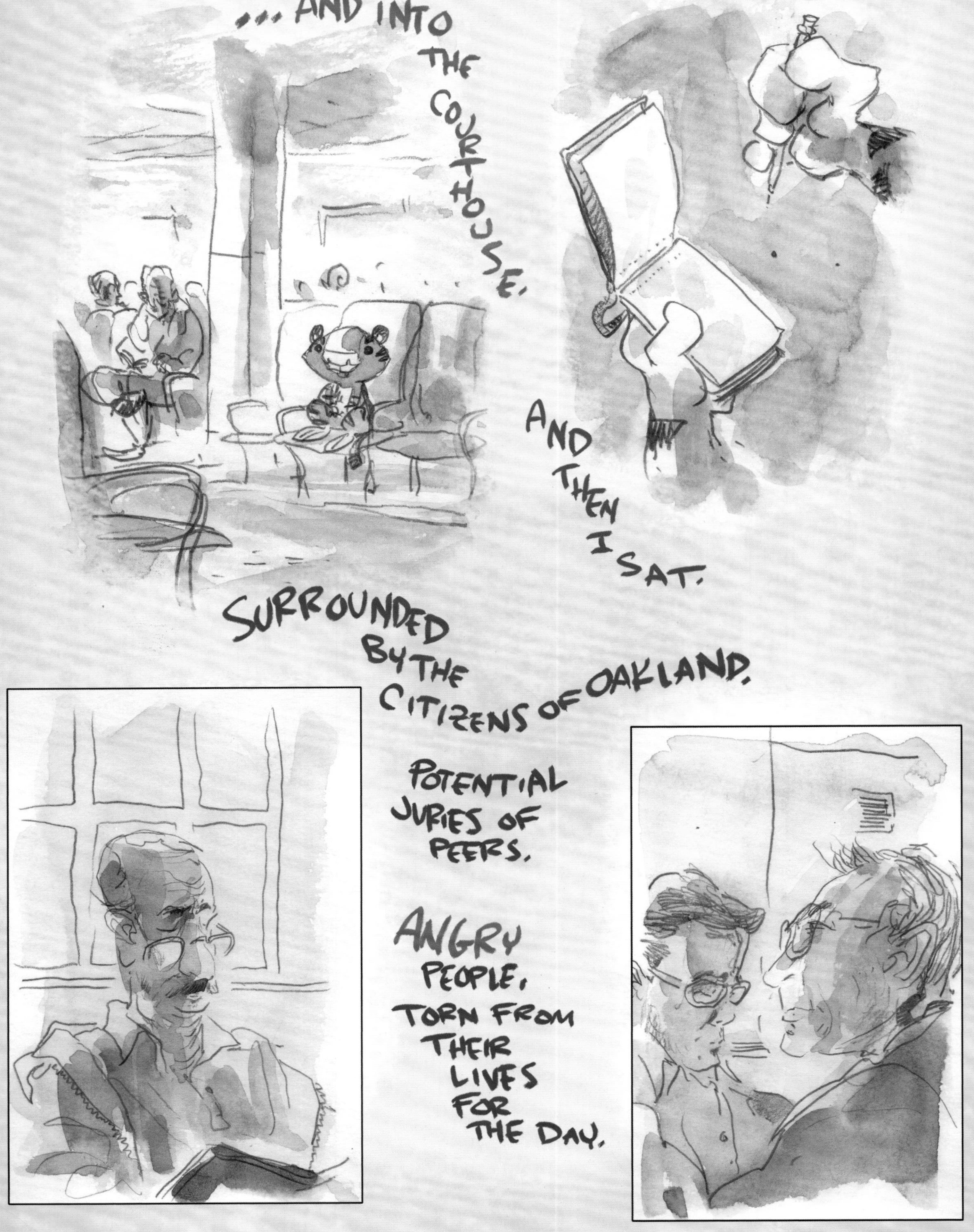
...AND INTO THE COURTHOUSE.
AND THEN I SAT.
SURROUNDED BY THE CITIZENS OF OAKLAND.
POTENTIAL JURIES OF PEERS.
ANGRY PEOPLE, TORN FROM THEIR LIVES FOR THE DAY.

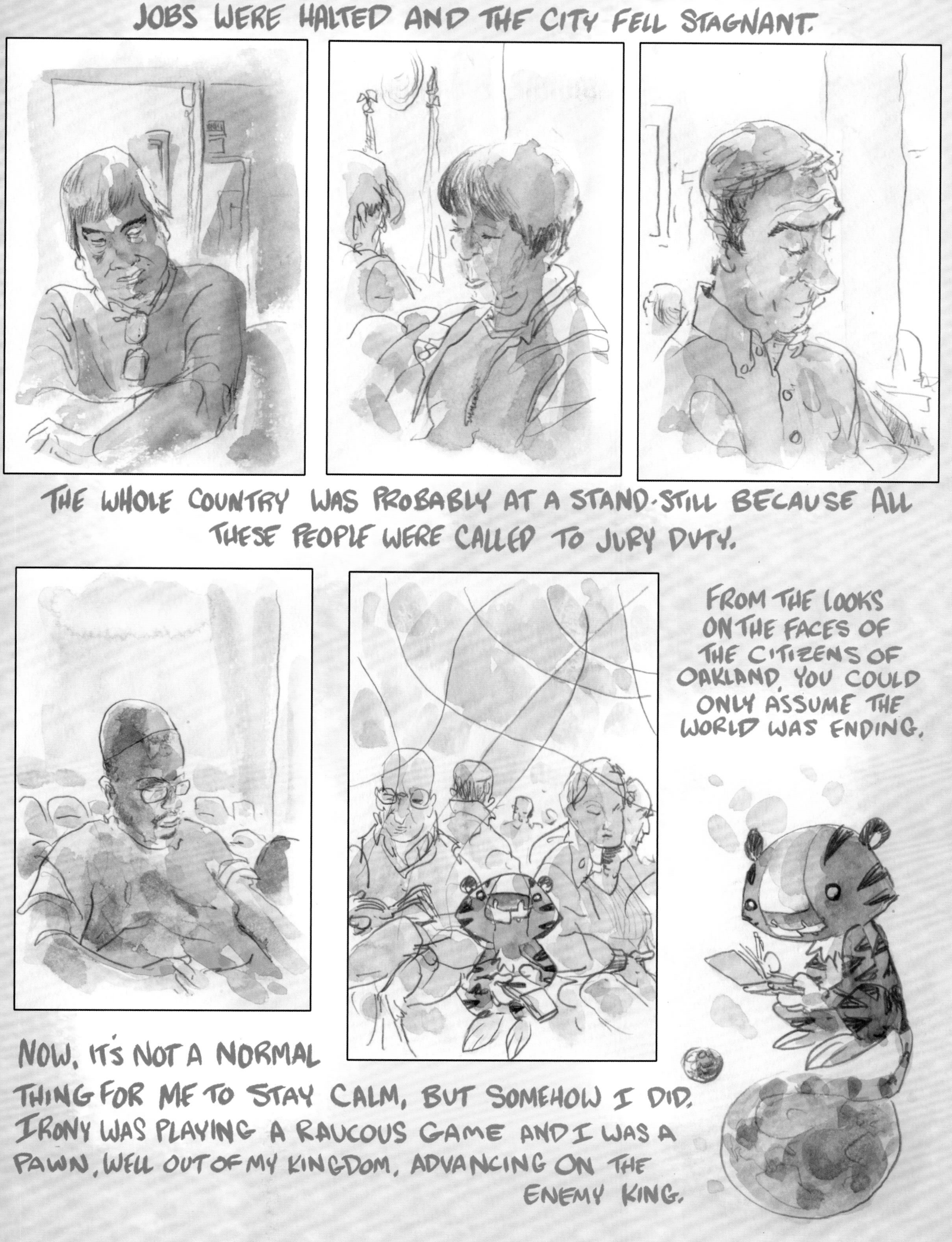
JOBS WERE HALTED AND THE CITY FELL STAGNANT.
THE WHOLE COUNTRY WAS PROBABLY AT A STAND-STILL BECAUSE ALL THESE PEOPLE WERE CALLED TO JURY DUTY.
FROM THE LOOKS ON THE FACES OF THE CITIZENS OF OAKLAND, YOU COULD ONLY ASSUME THE WORLD WAS ENDING.
NOW, IT'S NOT A NORMAL THING FOR ME TO STAY CALM, BUT SOMEHOW I DID. IRONY WAS PLAYING A RAUCOUS GAME AND I WAS A PAWN, WELL OUT OF MY KINGDOM, ADVANCING ON THE ENEMY KING.

WHILE ACTUALLY SINGLED OUT
AND SUMMONED TO THE COURTHOUSE
BY *NAME*, I COULD ESSENTIALLY
ESCAPE THE WORLD FOR A DAY.

I WAS NOW A NUMBER,
NAMELESS. NO *REAL*
IDENTITY, AND VERY LITTLE
RESPONSIBILITY. UNLESS I GOT
PLACED ON A JURY.

THEY PUT ME IN 'GROUP TWO',
OF THREE. GROUP ONE LEFT
THE ROOM LIKE A PACK OF
ZOMBIES.

GROUP TWO WAS TOLD
THEY WOULDN'T BE NEEDED
UNTIL AFTER LUNCH.
WE WERE FREE TO GO
FOR HOURS,

FREE!

SO I ROAMED
DOWNTOWN
OAKLAND.

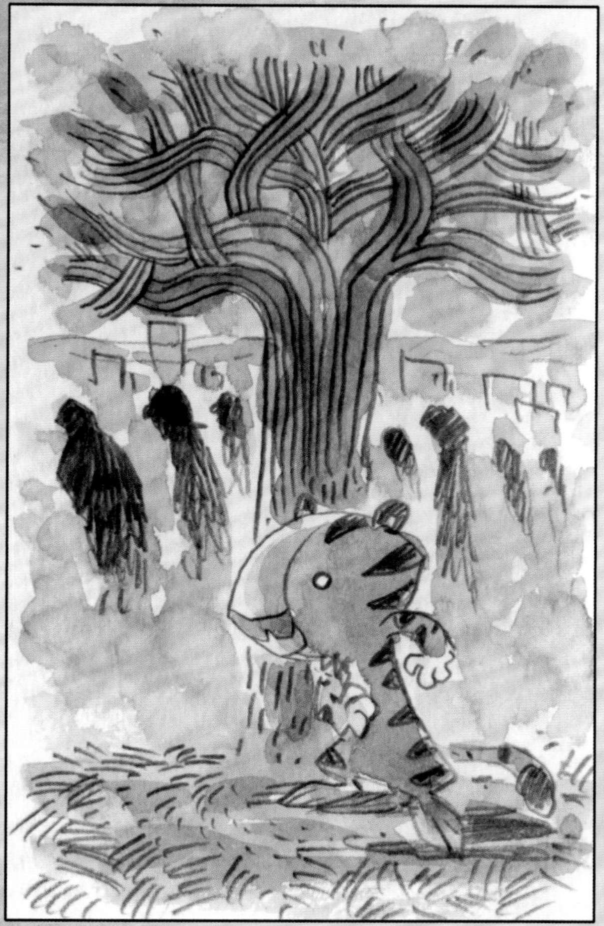

OAKLAND WAS A PLACE THAT, AS A KID, I'D NEVER *DREAM* OF ROAMING ON FOOT.

YOU SIMPLY DIDN'T GO TO OAKLAND.

PEOPLE WERE SHOT AND KILLED IN *OAKLAND*.

YOU SURE AS *HELL* WOULDN'T LIVE THERE.

I'VE LEARNED A LOT SINCE THEN, AND MY 'SURENESS' OF *HELL* HAS DWINDLED.

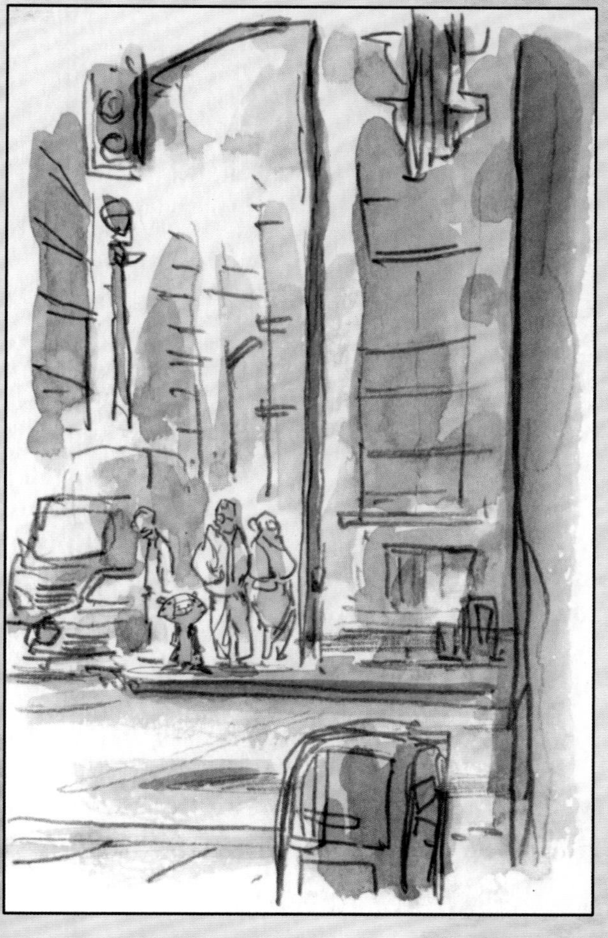

OAKLAND, OF ALL PLACES, HAS SOMEHOW BECOME MY *HOME*.

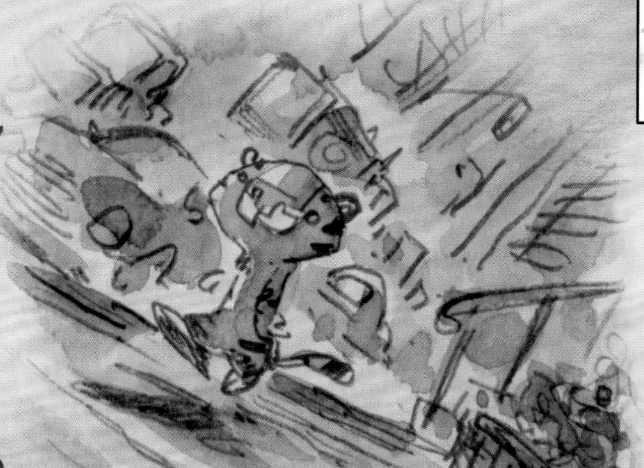

I'M A *CITIZEN* OF OAKLAND.

I FIND VERY LITTLE *FEAR* ON THE STREETS.

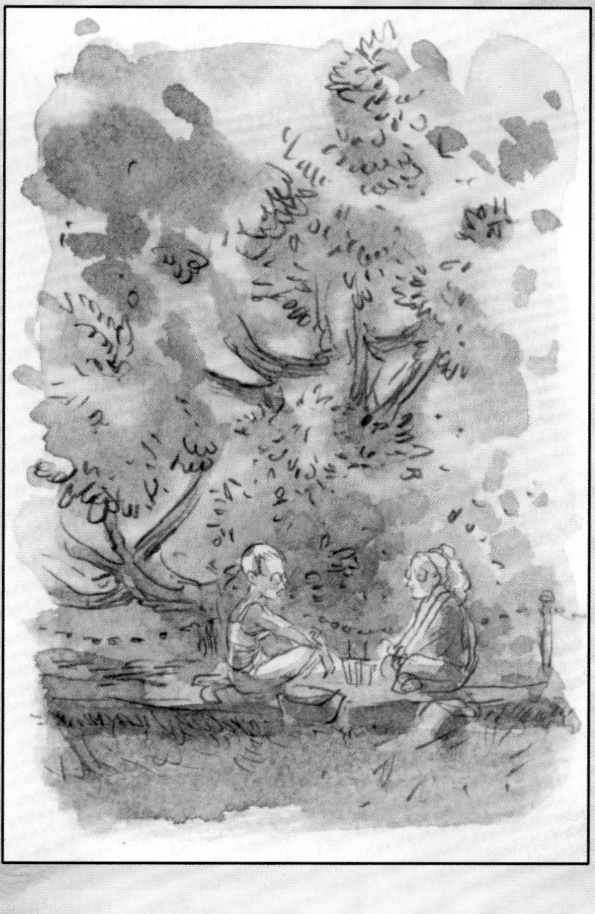

NEIGHBORHOODS ARE ANOTHER STORY, BUT THE STREETS OF DOWNTOWN ARE ACTUALLY PRETTY QUIET IN THE DAYLIGHT.

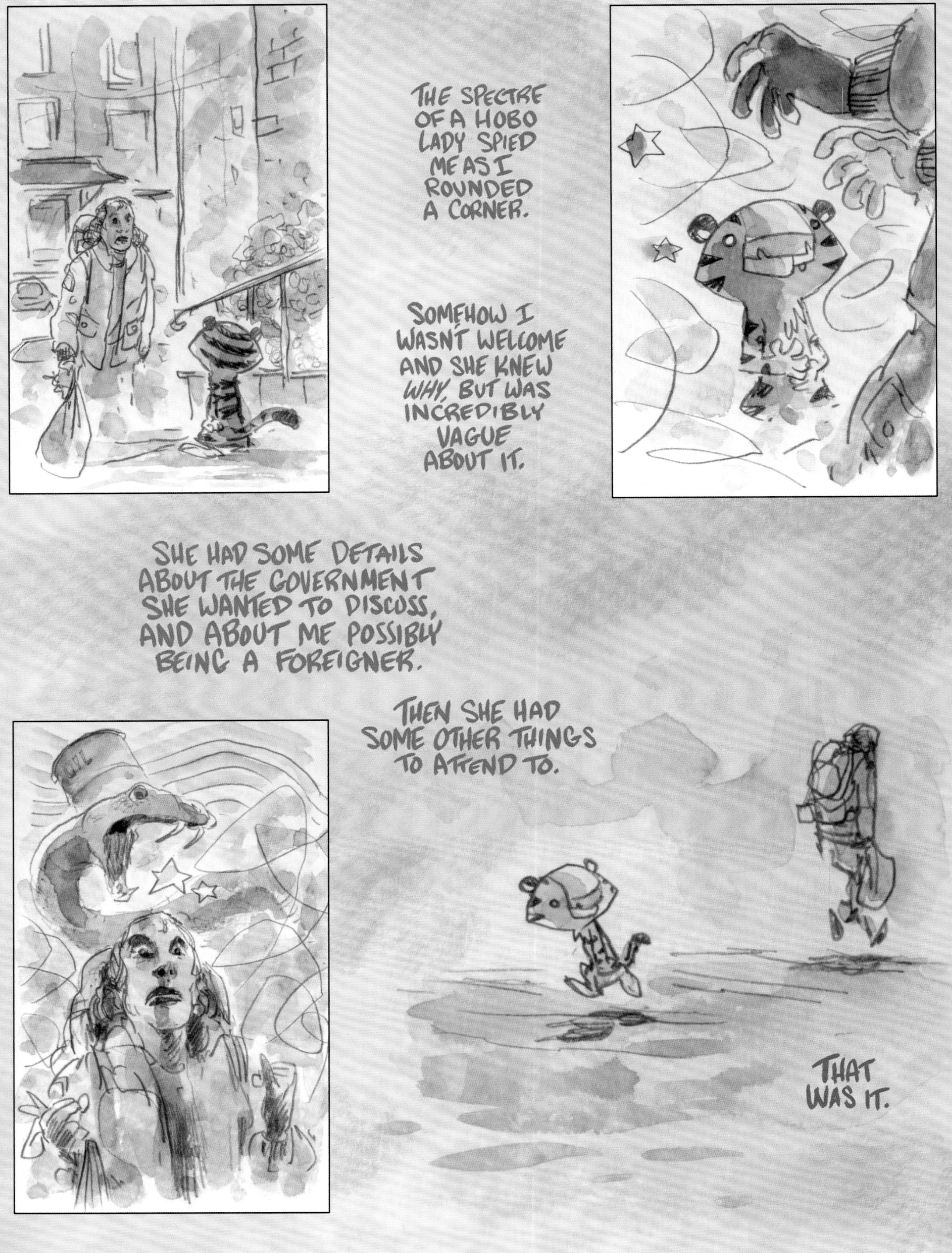
THE SPECTRE OF A HOBO LADY SPIED ME AS I ROUNDED A CORNER.
SOMEHOW I WASN'T WELCOME AND SHE KNEW *WHY*, BUT WAS INCREDIBLY VAGUE ABOUT IT.
SHE HAD SOME DETAILS ABOUT THE GOVERNMENT SHE WANTED TO DISCUSS, AND ABOUT ME POSSIBLY BEING A FOREIGNER.
THEN SHE HAD SOME OTHER THINGS TO ATTEND TO.
THAT WAS IT.

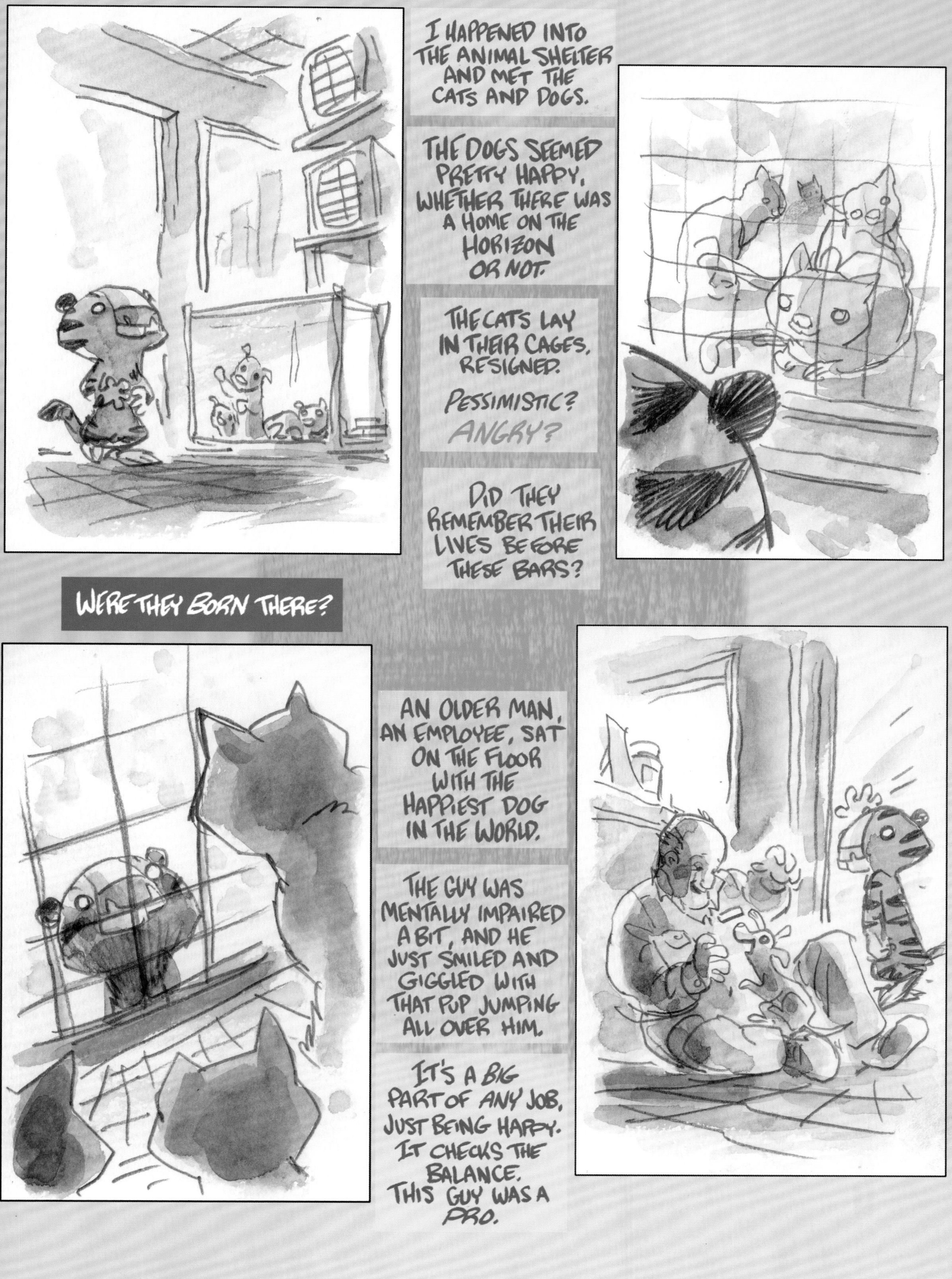
I HAPPENED INTO THE ANIMAL SHELTER AND MET THE CATS AND DOGS.
THE DOGS SEEMED PRETTY HAPPY, WHETHER THERE WAS A HOME ON THE HORIZON OR NOT.
THE CATS LAY IN THEIR CAGES, RESIGNED.
PESSIMISTIC?
ANGRY?
DID THEY REMEMBER THEIR LIVES BEFORE THESE BARS?
WERE THEY BORN THERE?
AN OLDER MAN, AN EMPLOYEE, SAT ON THE FLOOR WITH THE HAPPIEST DOG IN THE WORLD.
THE GUY WAS MENTALLY IMPAIRED A BIT, AND HE JUST SMILED AND GIGGLED WITH THAT PUP JUMPING ALL OVER HIM.
IT'S A BIG PART OF ANY JOB, JUST BEING HAPPY. IT CHECKS THE BALANCE. THIS GUY WAS A PRO.

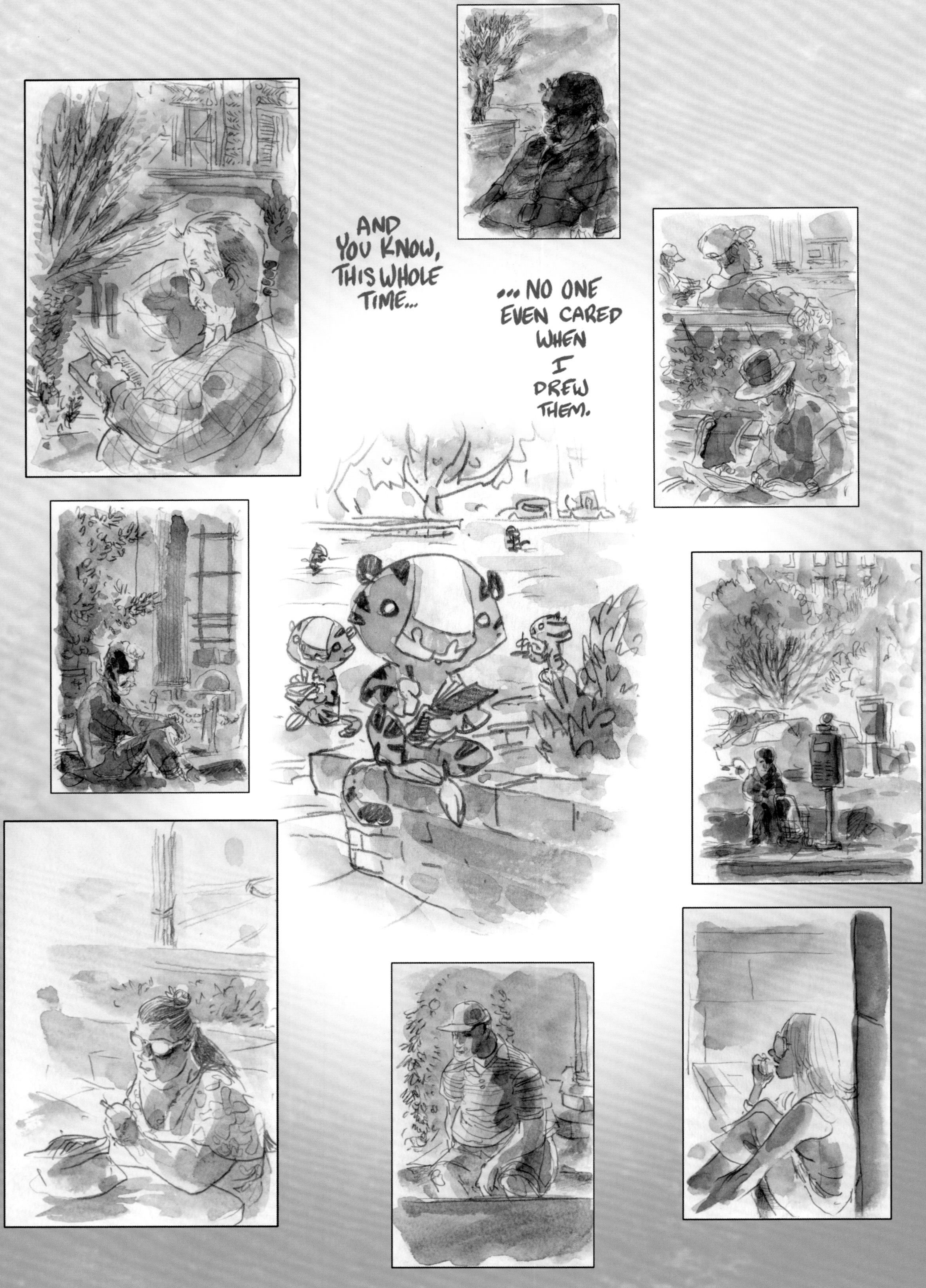
AND YOU KNOW, THIS WHOLE TIME...
...NO ONE EVEN CARED WHEN I DREW THEM.

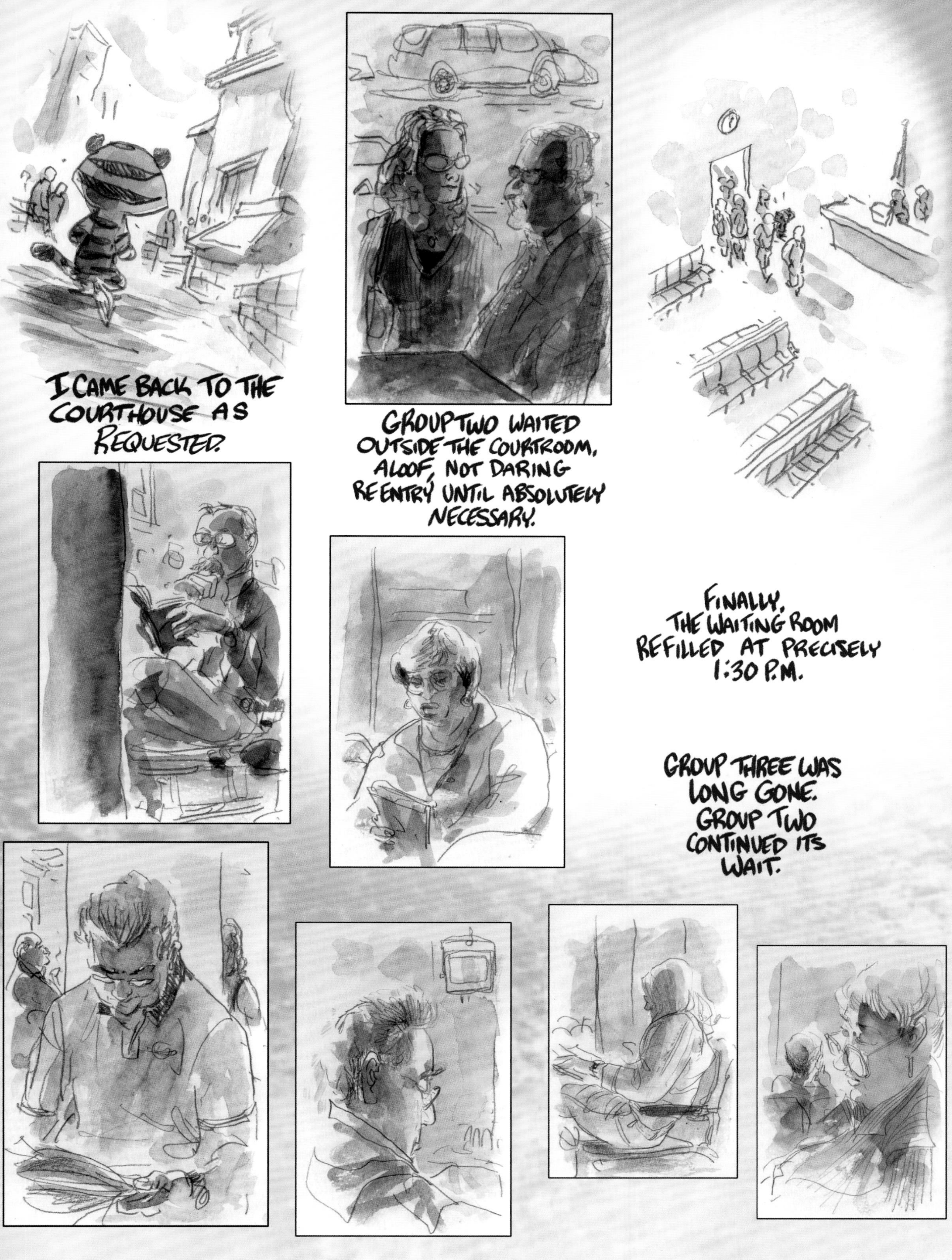
I CAME BACK TO THE COURTHOUSE AS REQUESTED.
GROUP TWO WAITED OUTSIDE THE COURTROOM, ALOOF, NOT DARING REENTRY UNTIL ABSOLUTELY NECESSARY.
FINALLY, THE WAITING ROOM REFILLED AT PRECISELY 1:30 P.M.
GROUP THREE WAS LONG GONE. GROUP TWO CONTINUED ITS WAIT.

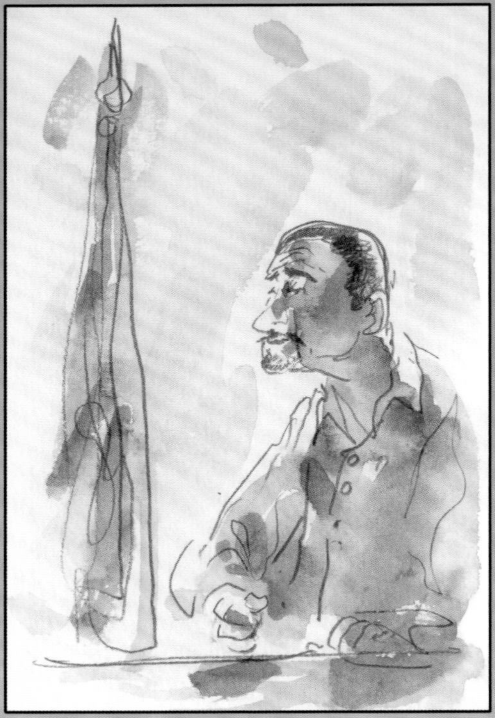

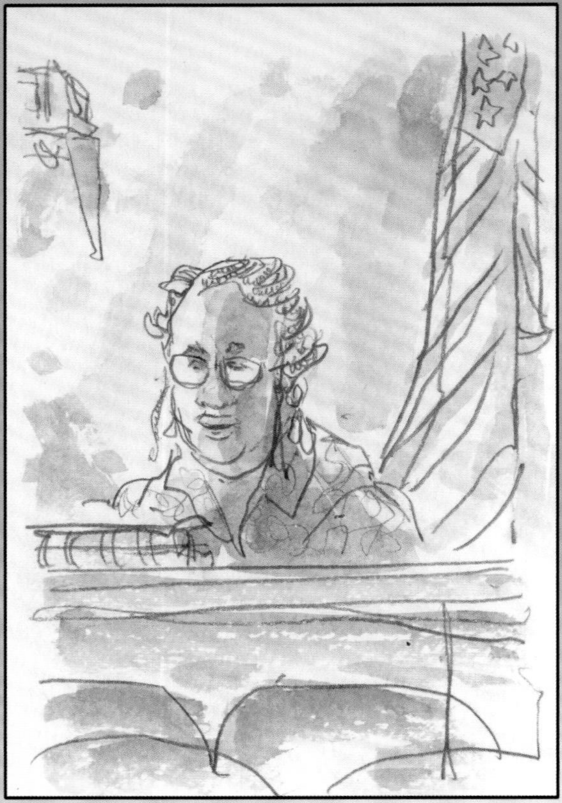

SUDDENLY, NAMES WERE CALLED.

A FIRING SQUAD WAS UNDOUBTEDLY STATIONED JUST OUTSIDE, WAITING FOR US.

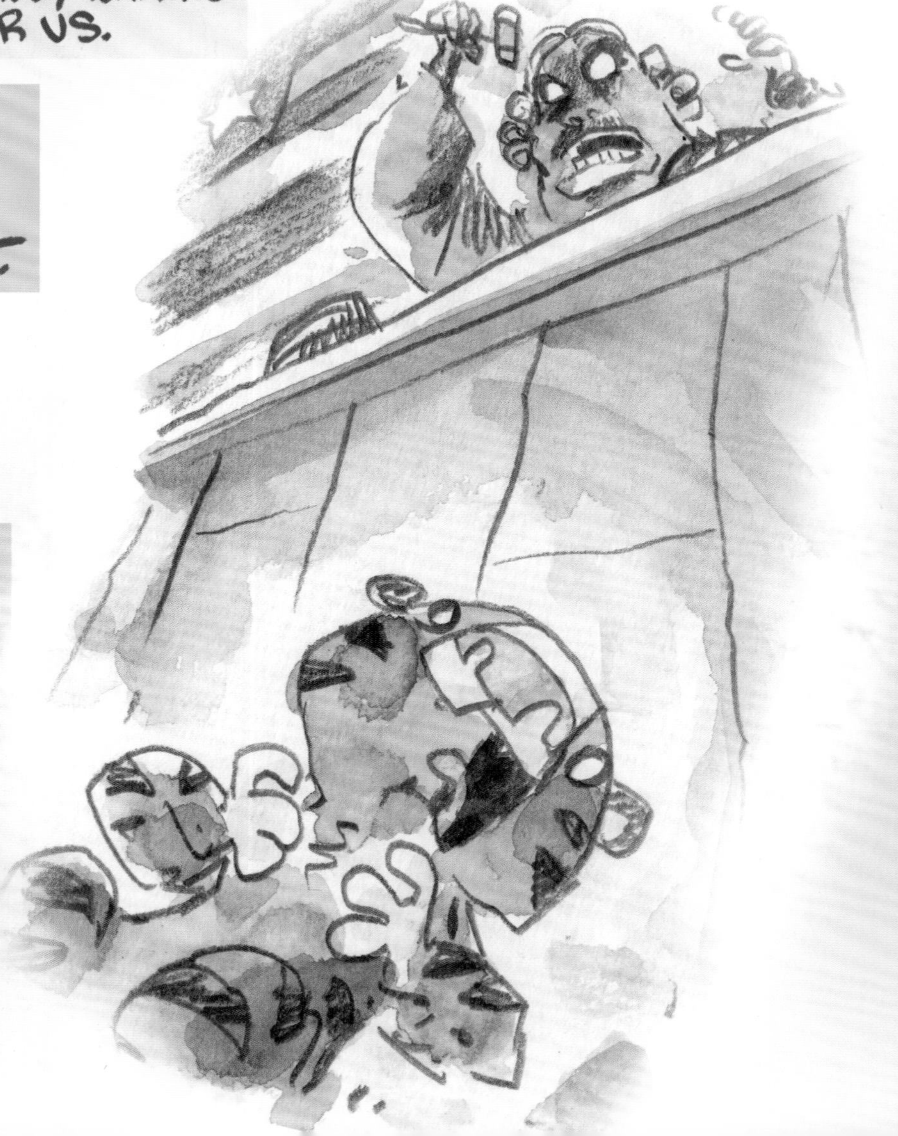

NOW THE **TERROR** WOULD ERRUPT.

THIS WAS THE *COURT.*

I WOULD THROW MYSELF AT ITS MERCY, A *MARTYR*, THANKFUL FOR THE LAST FEW HOURS OF FREEDOM THAT THE COURT HAD GIVEN ME.

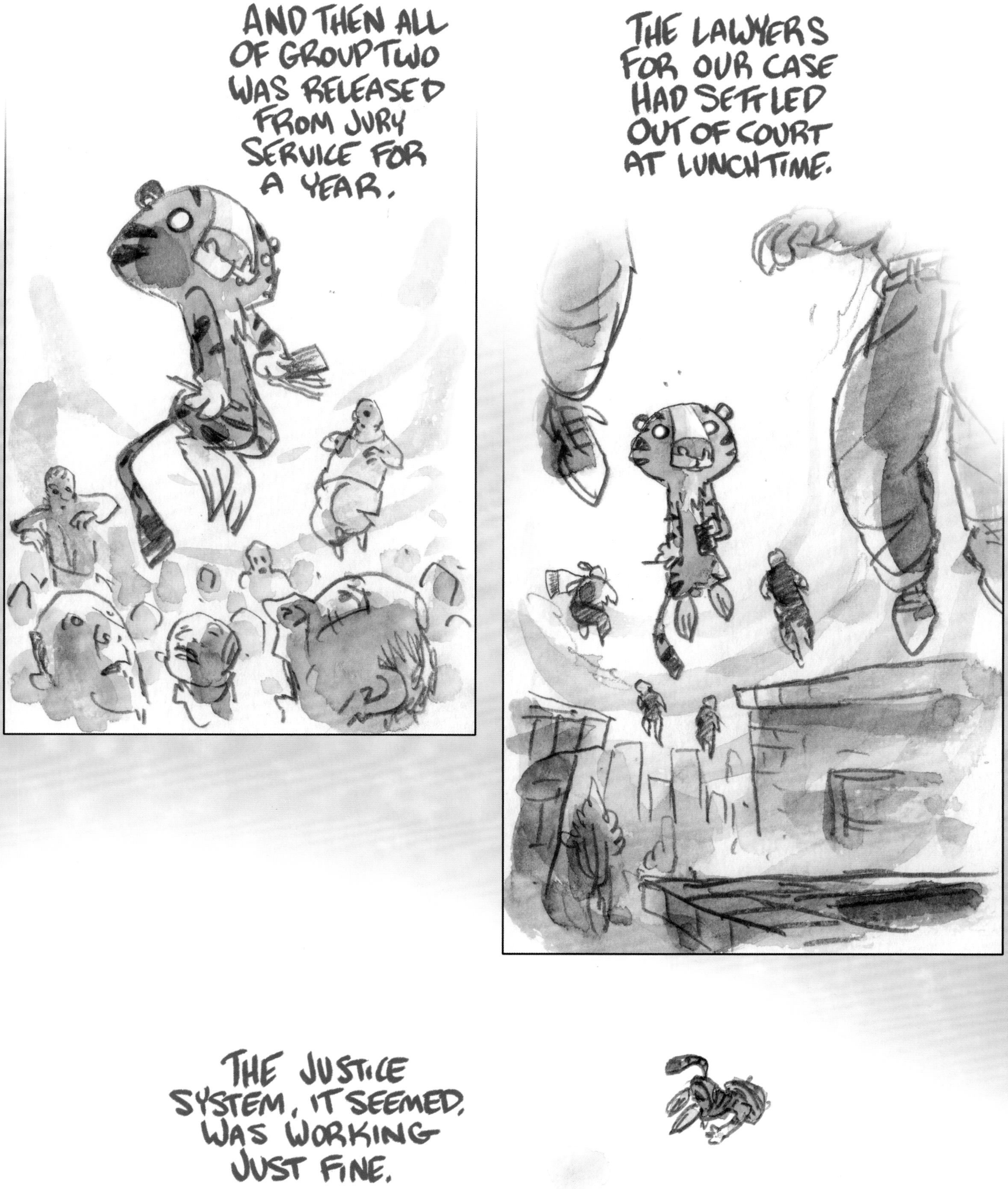
AND THEN ALL OF GROUP TWO WAS RELEASED FROM JURY SERVICE FOR A YEAR.
THE LAWYERS FOR OUR CASE HAD SETTLED OUT OF COURT AT LUNCHTIME.
THE JUSTICE SYSTEM, IT SEEMED, WAS WORKING JUST FINE.

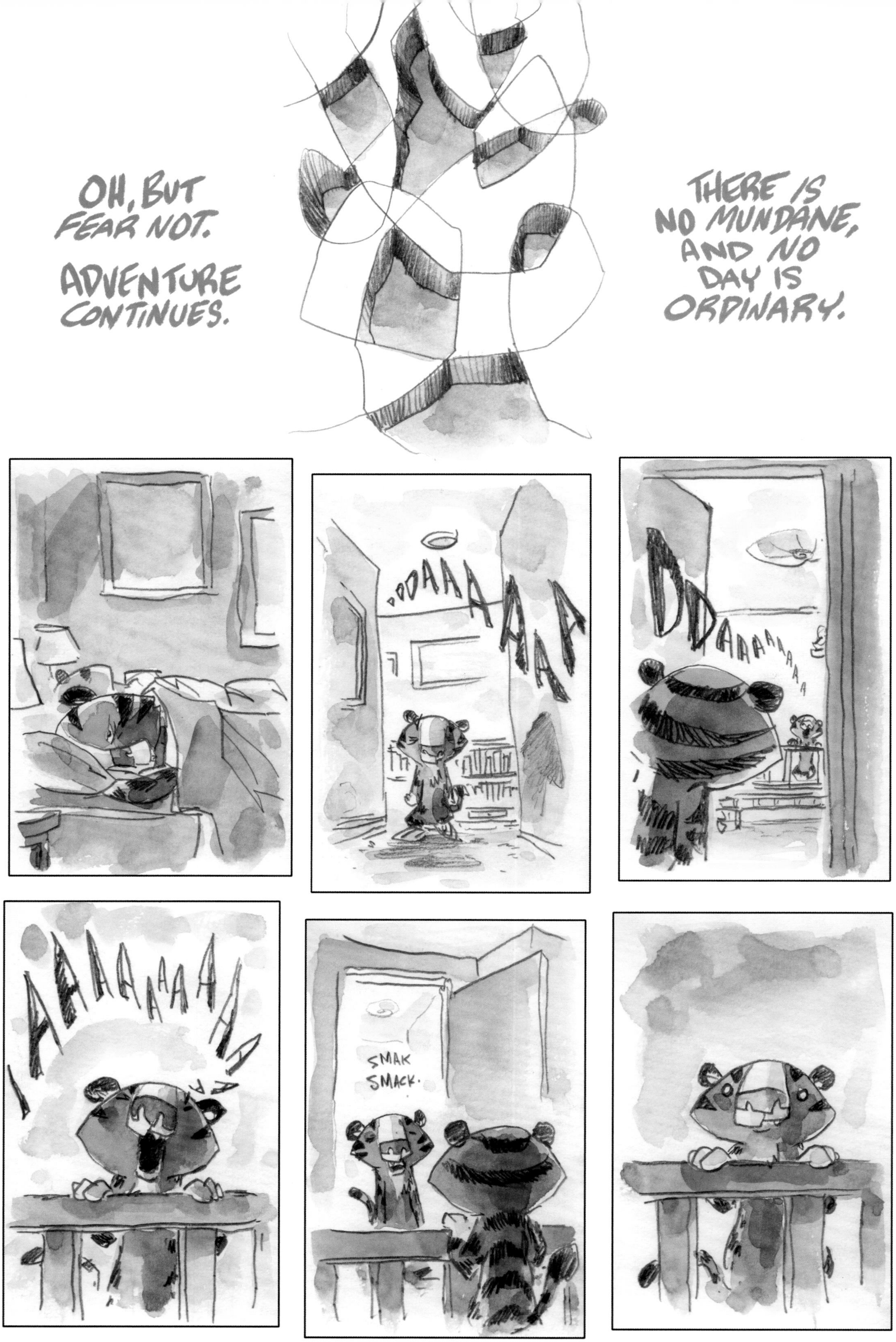
OH, BUT FEAR NOT.
ADVENTURE CONTINUES.
THERE IS NO MUNDANE, AND NO DAY IS ORDINARY.
SMAK
SMACK.

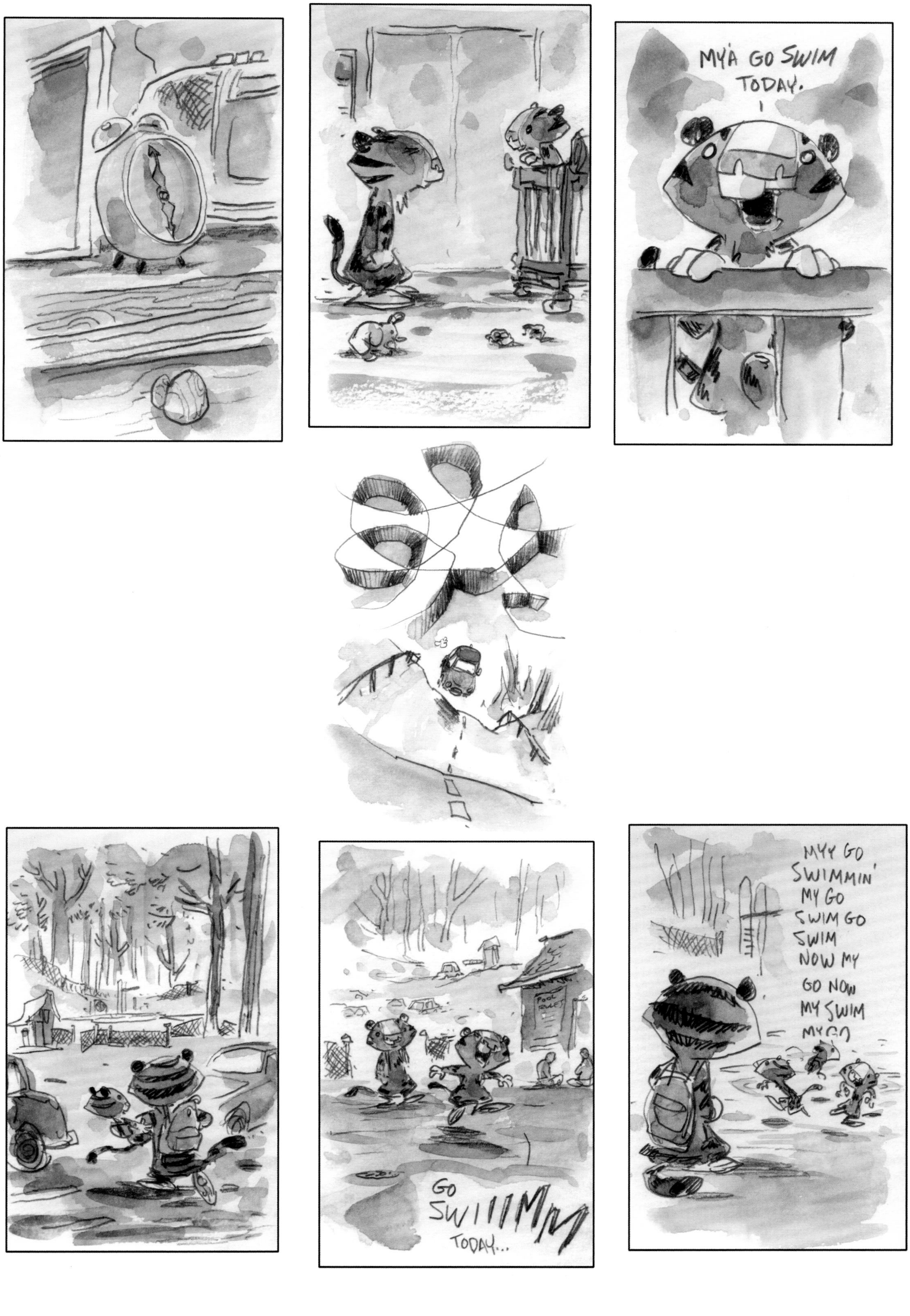
MY'A GO SWIM TODAY.
GO SWIIIMM TODAY...
MYY GO SWIMMIN' MY GO SWIM GO SWIM NOW MY GO NOW MY SWIM MY GO

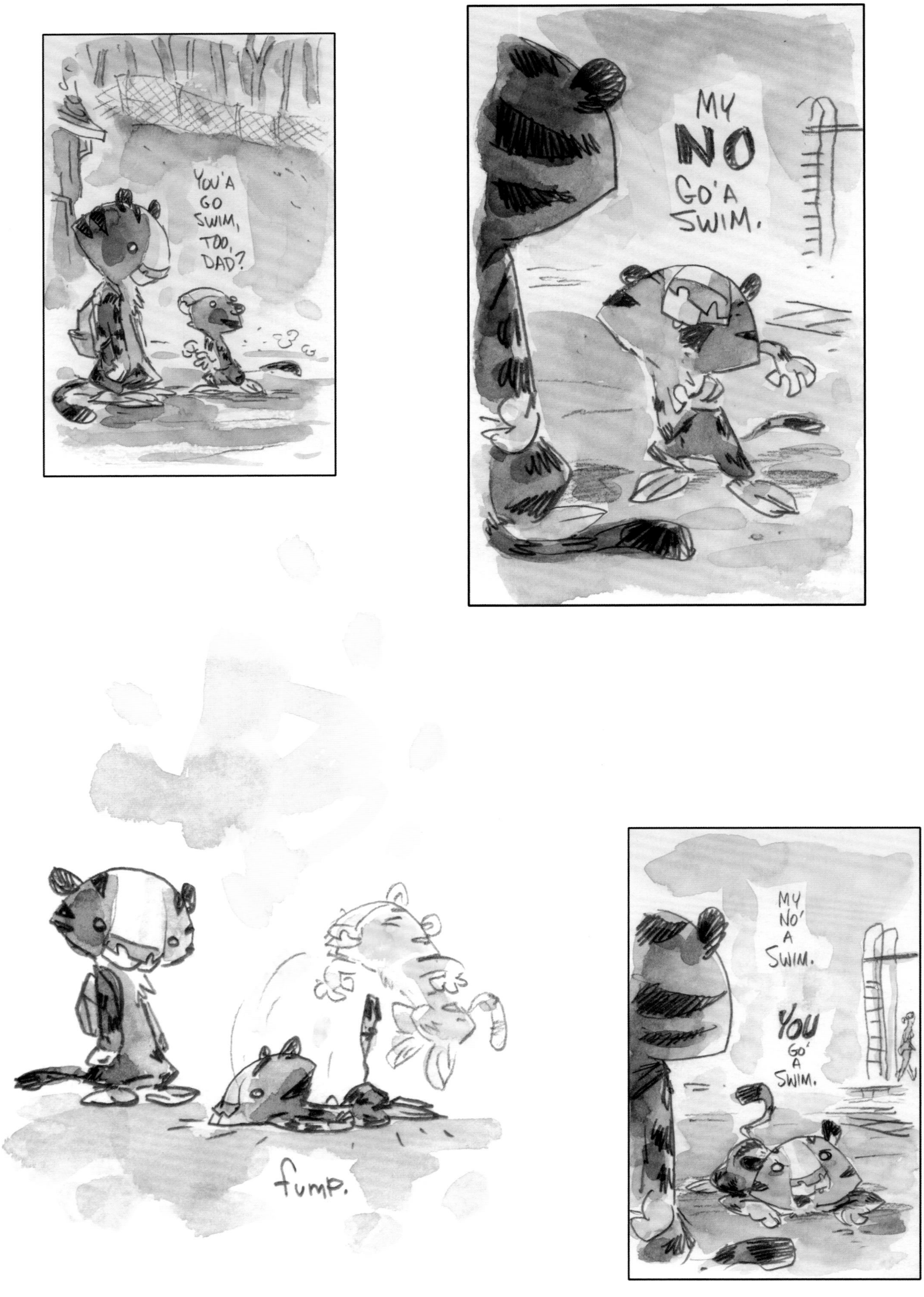
YOU'A GO SWIM, TOO, DAD?
MY NO GO'A SWIM.
fump.
MY NO' A SWIM.
YOU GO' A SWIM.

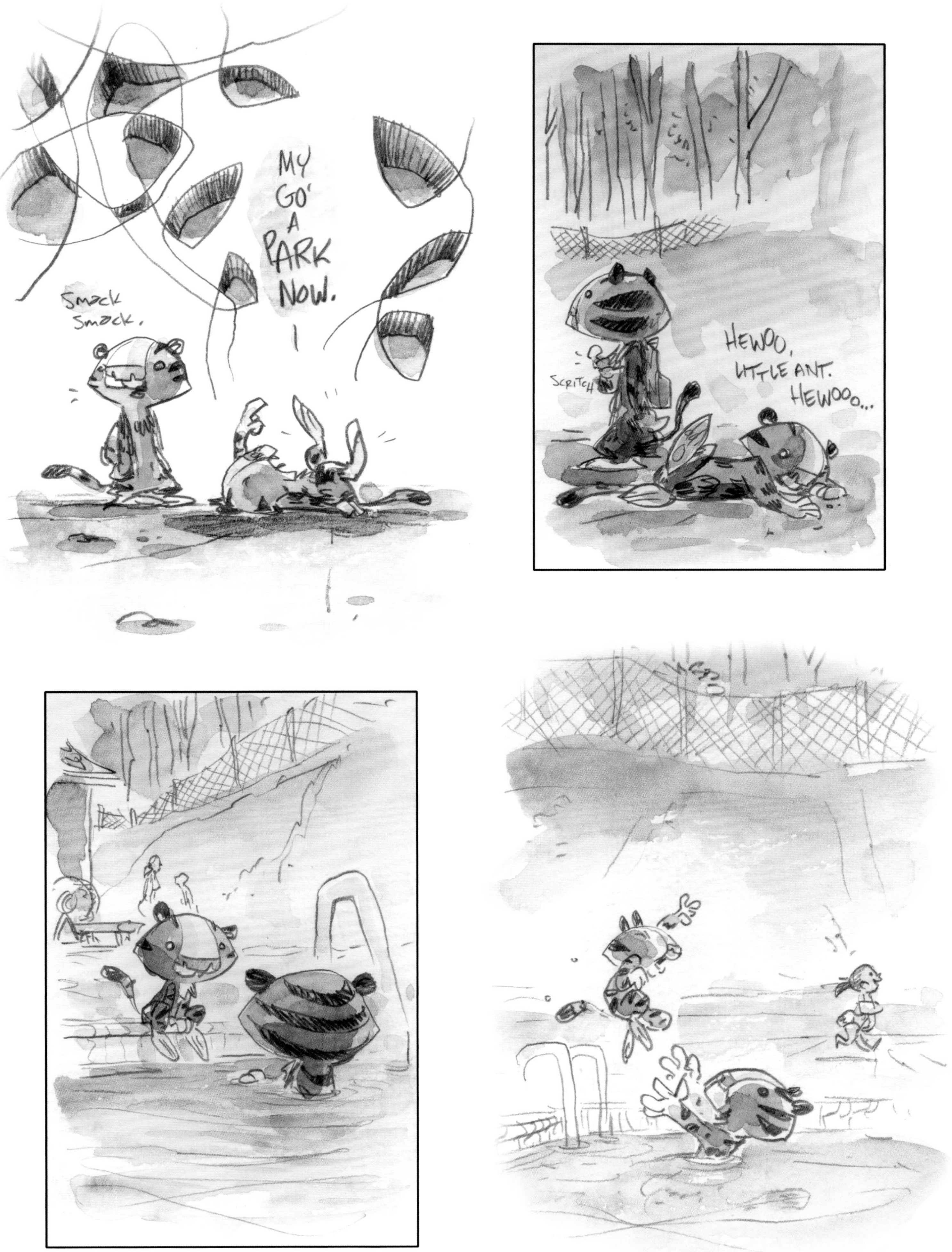
Smack Smack.
MY GO' A PARK NOW.
SCRITCH
HEWOO, LITTLE ANT. HEWOOO...

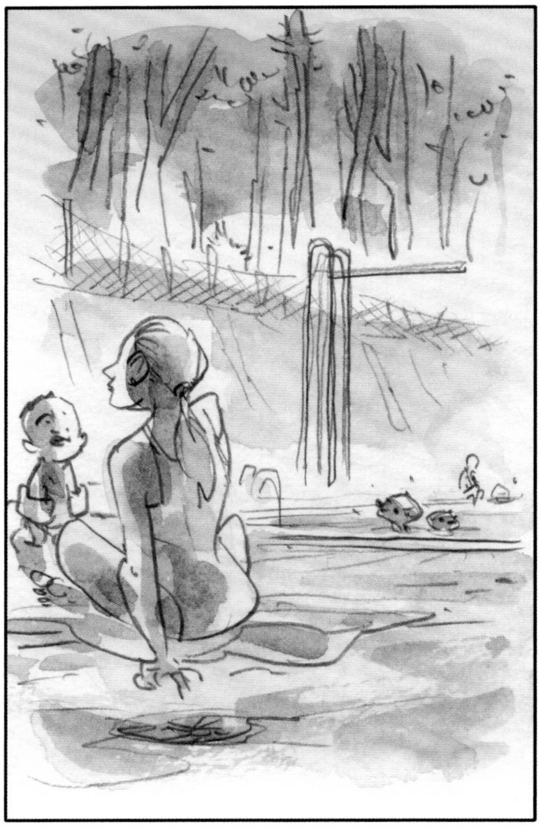

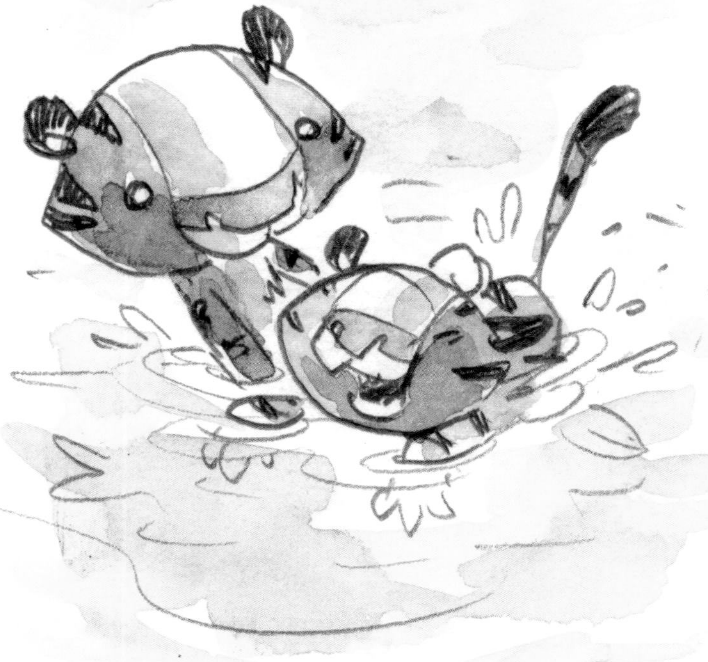

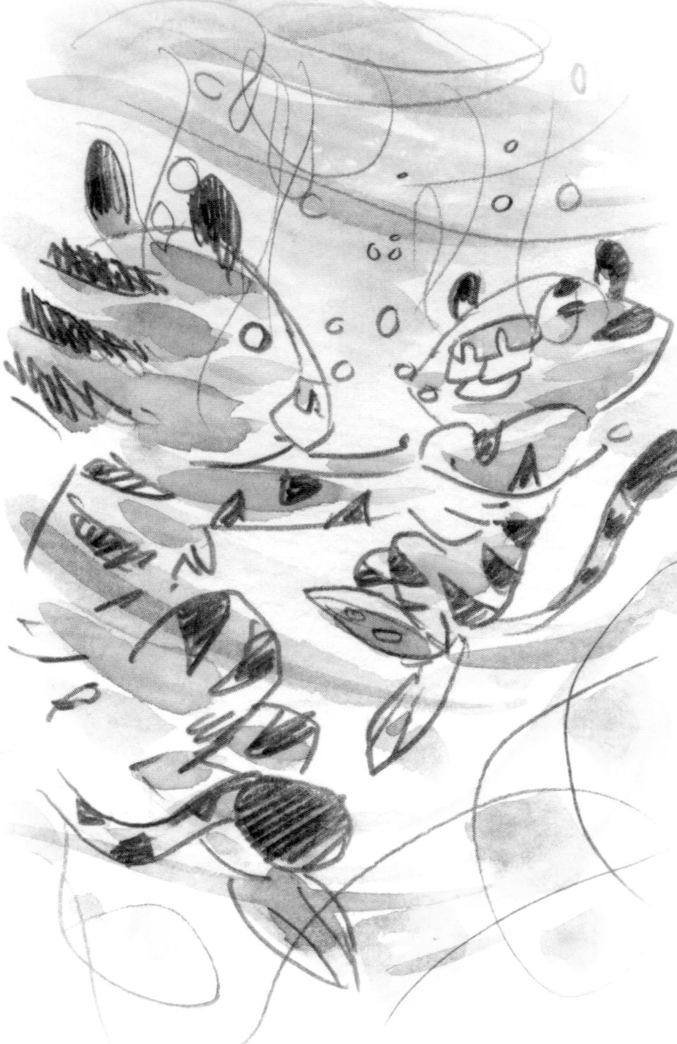

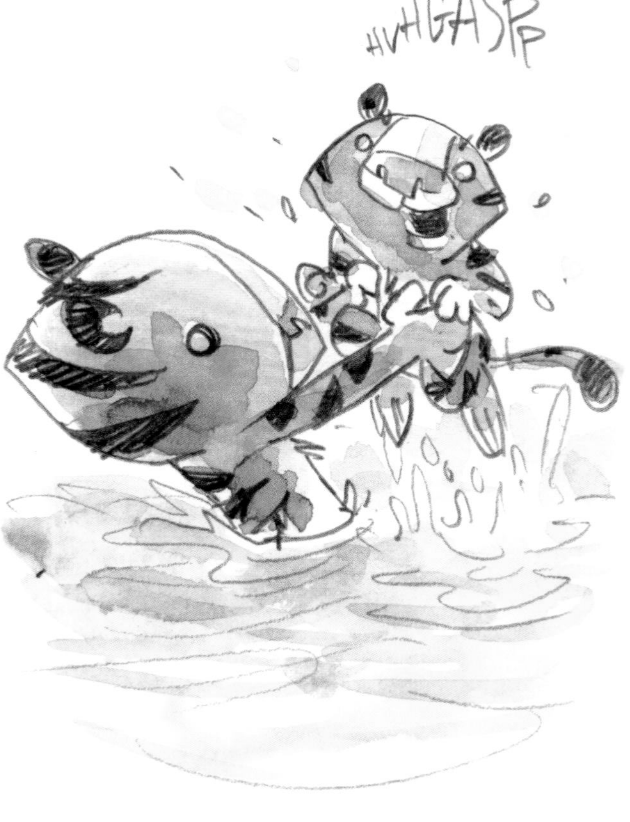
HUHGASPP

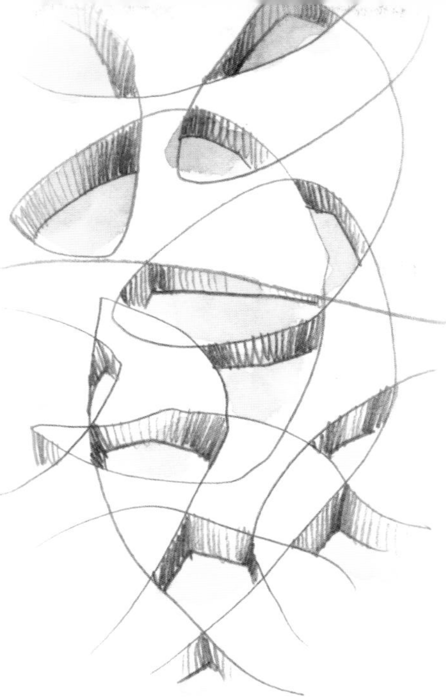

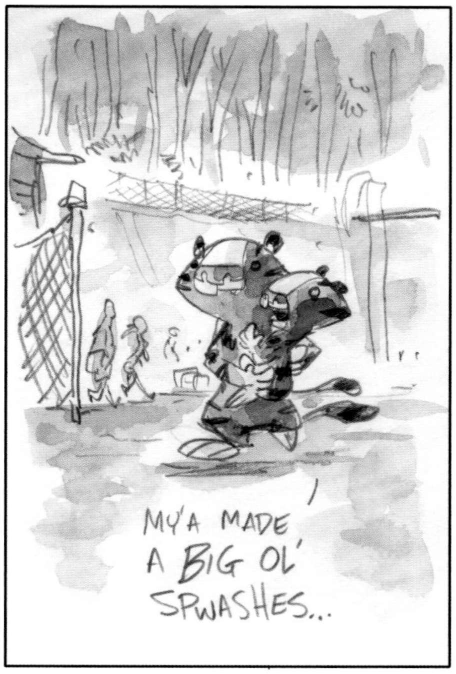
MY'A MADE A BIG OL' SPWASHES...

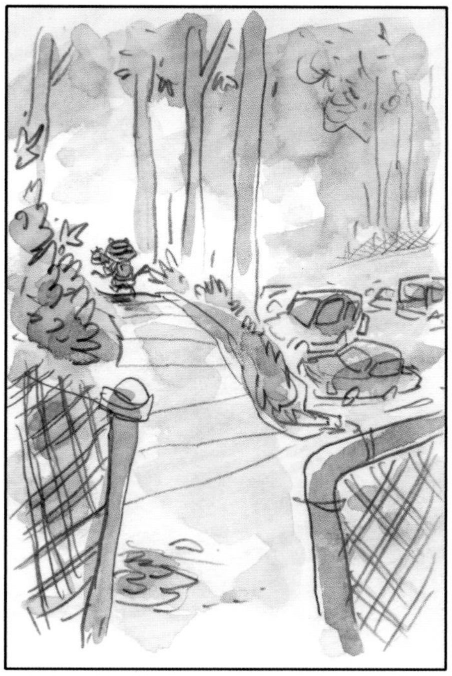

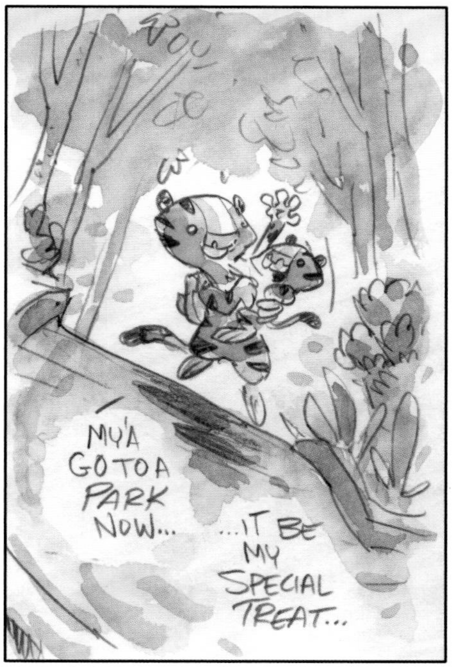
MY'A GO TO A PARK NOW...
...IT BE MY SPECIAL TREAT...

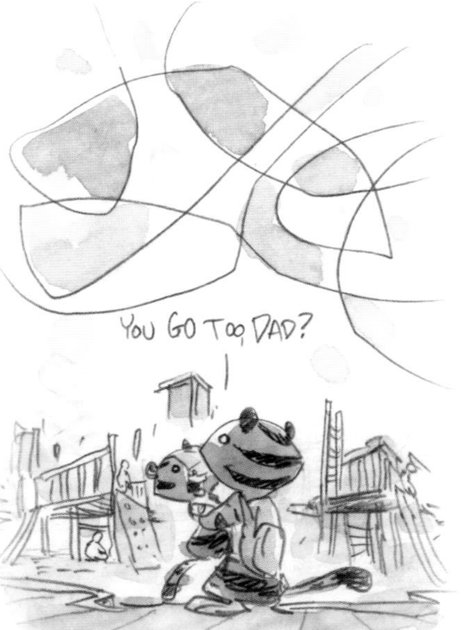
YOU GO TOO, DAD?

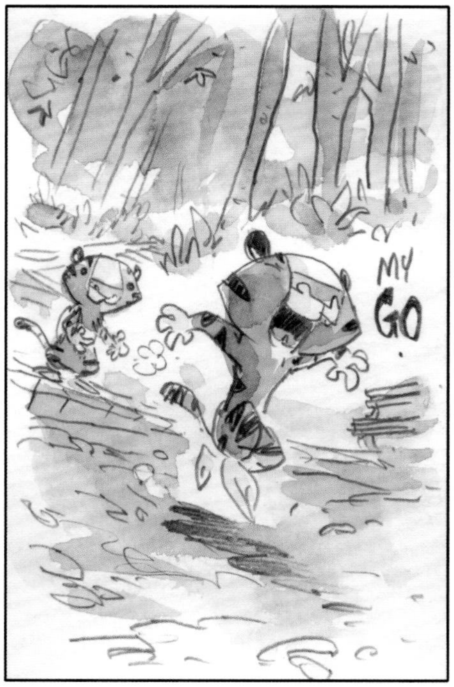
MY GO

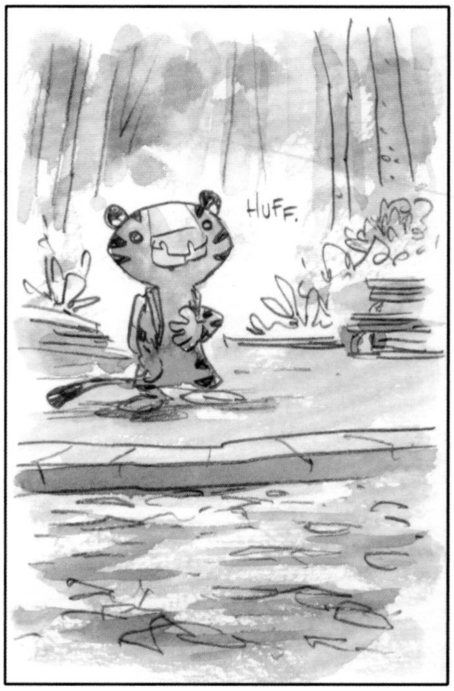
HUFF.

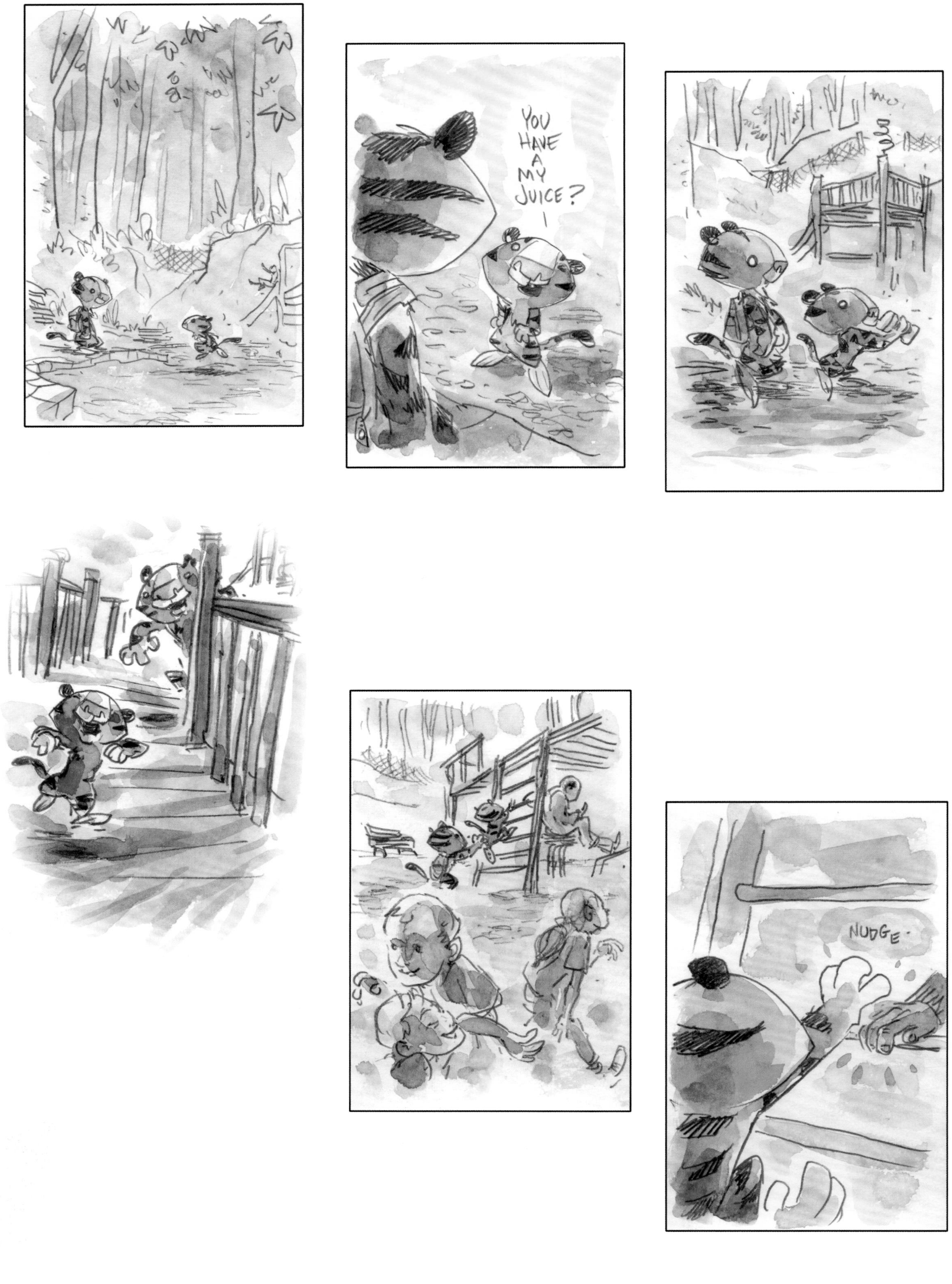
YOU HAVE A MY JUICE?
NUDGE

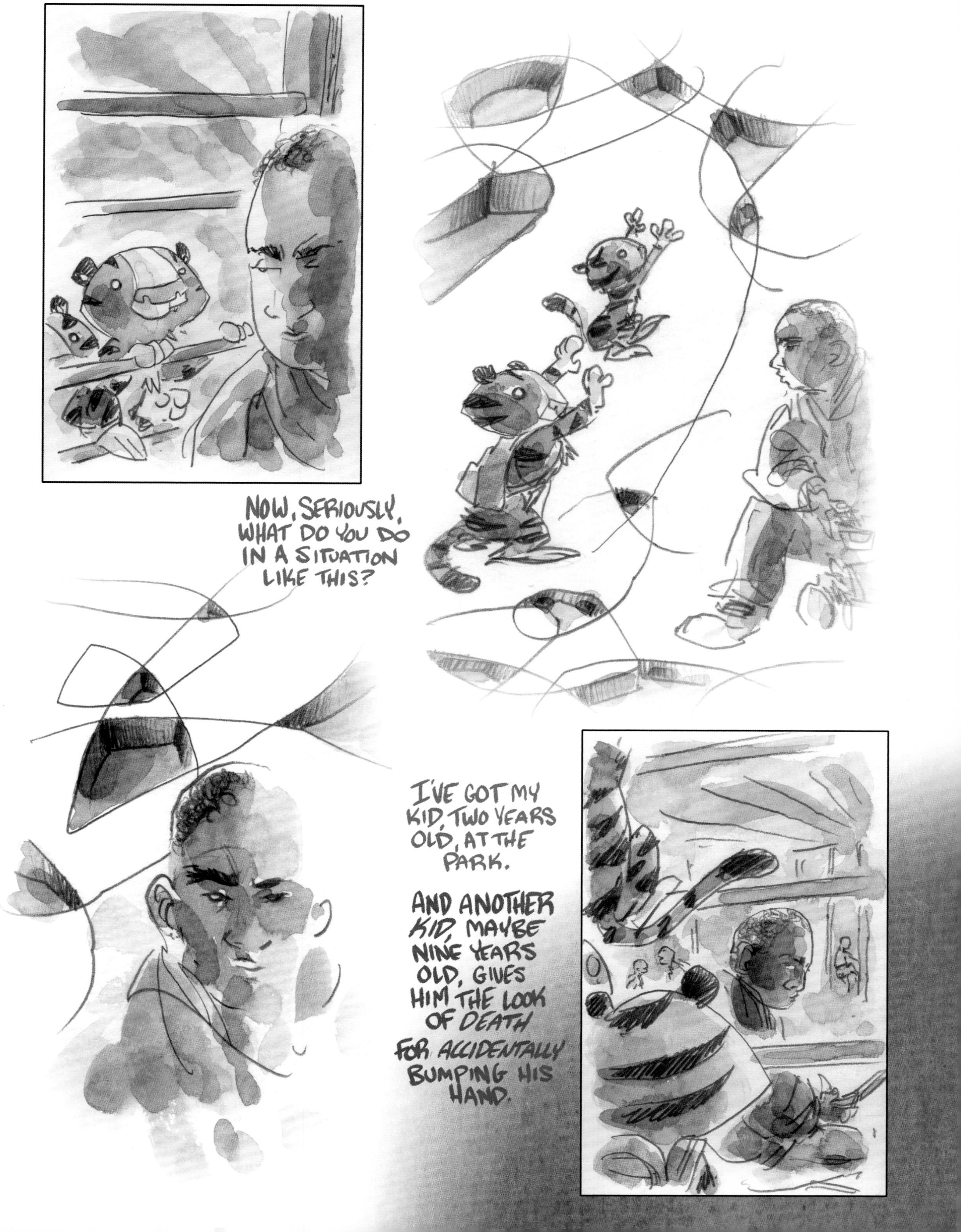
NOW, SERIOUSLY, WHAT DO YOU DO IN A SITUATION LIKE THIS?
I'VE GOT MY KID, TWO YEARS OLD, AT THE PARK.
AND ANOTHER KID, MAYBE NINE YEARS OLD, GIVES HIM THE LOOK OF DEATH
FOR ACCIDENTALLY BUMPING HIS HAND.

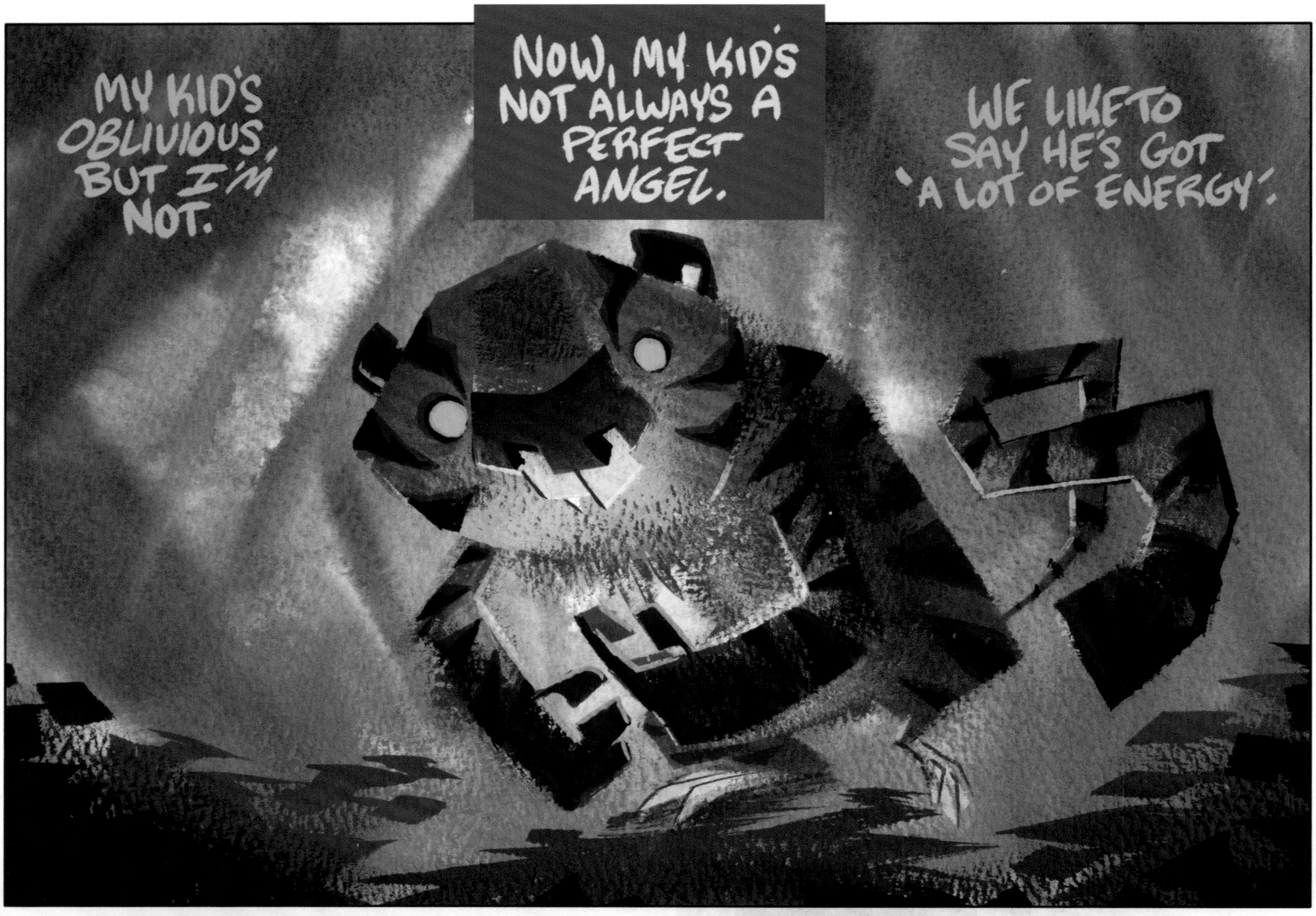
MY KID'S OBLIVIOUS, BUT I'M NOT.
NOW, MY KID'S NOT ALWAYS A PERFECT ANGEL.
WE LIKE TO SAY HE'S GOT 'A LOT OF ENERGY'.

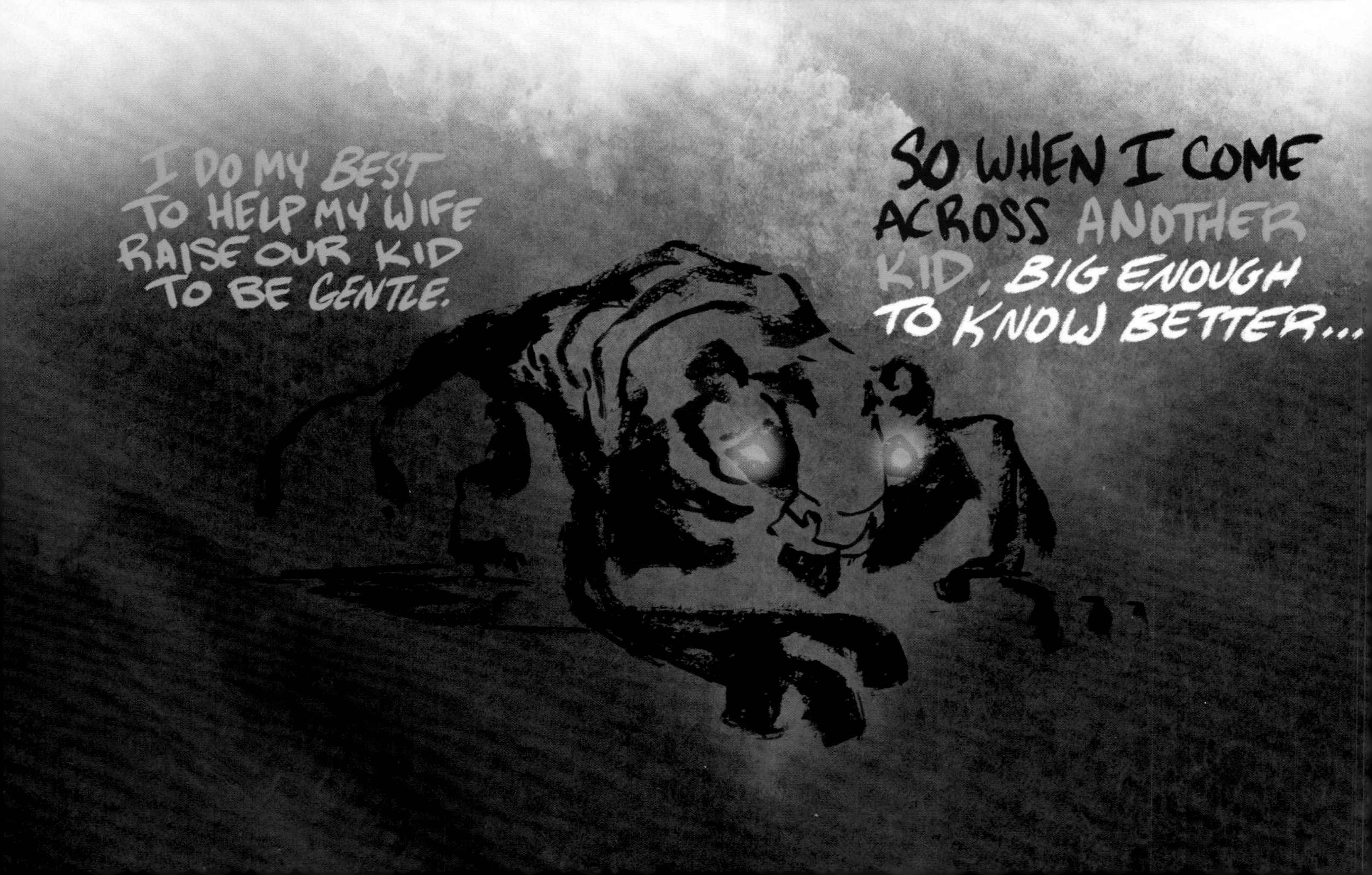
I DO MY BEST TO HELP MY WIFE RAISE OUR KID TO BE GENTLE.
SO WHEN I COME ACROSS ANOTHER KID, BIG ENOUGH TO KNOW BETTER...

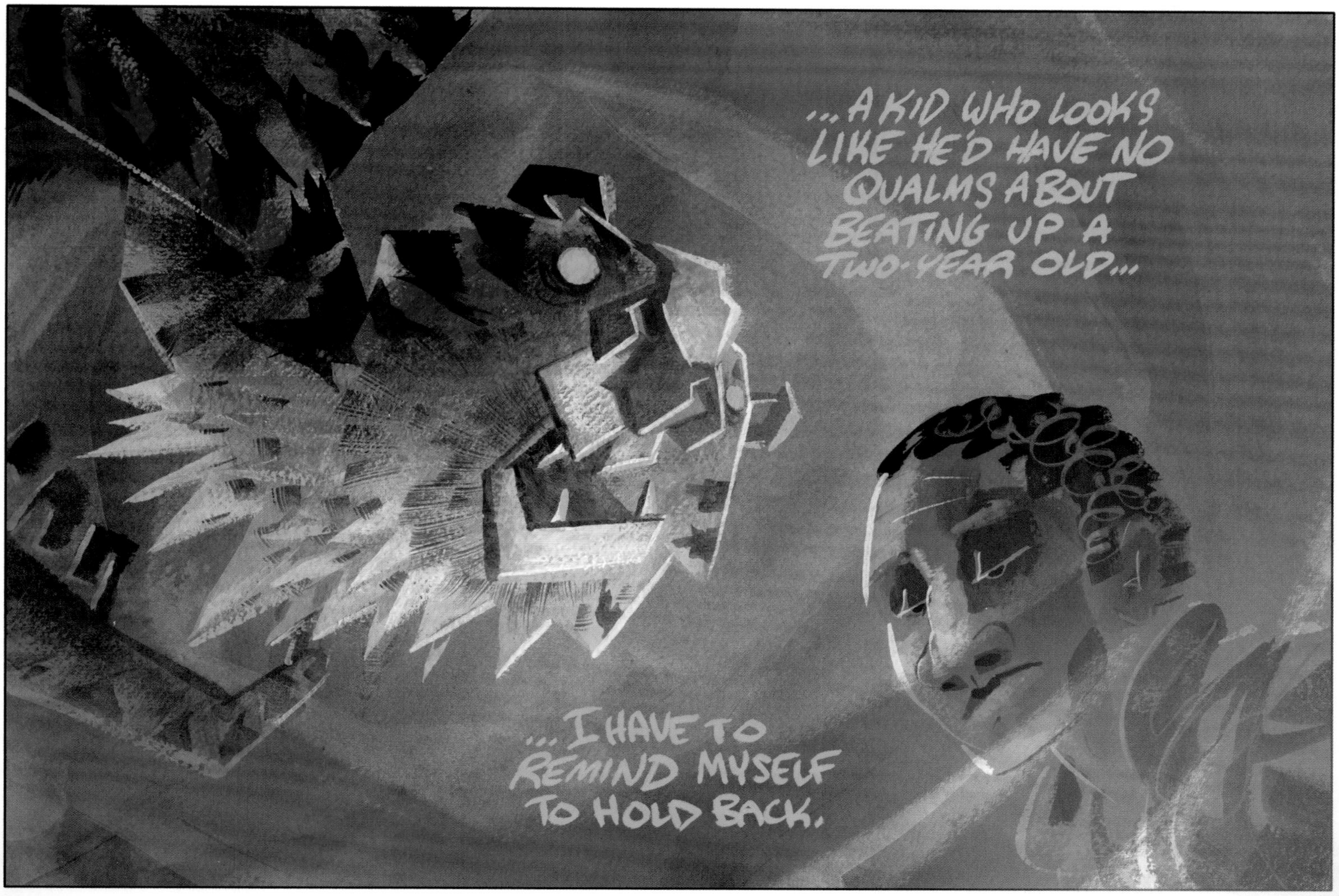
...A KID WHO LOOKS LIKE HE'D HAVE NO QUALMS ABOUT BEATING UP A TWO-YEAR OLD...
...I HAVE TO REMIND MYSELF TO HOLD BACK.

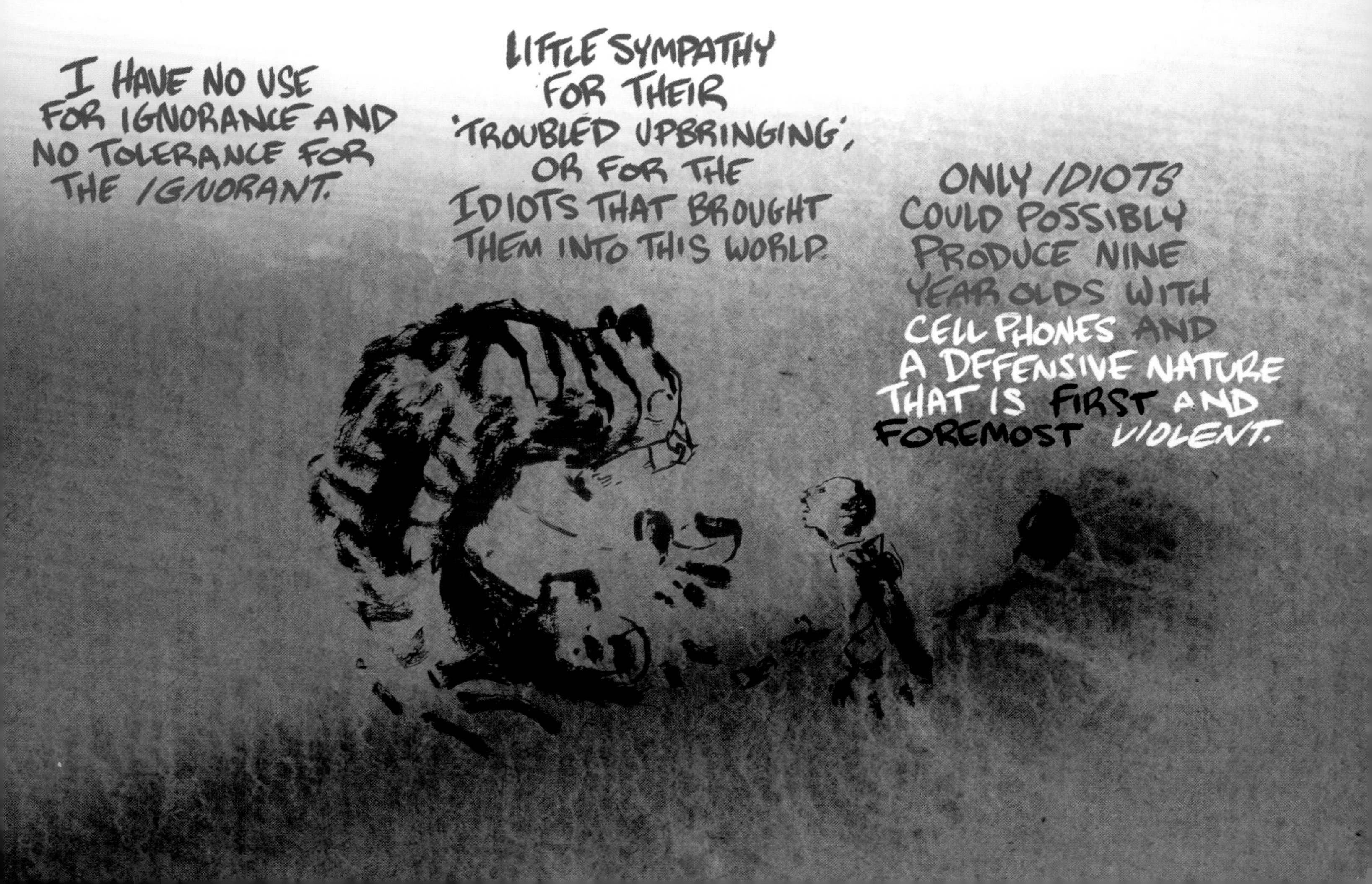
I HAVE NO USE FOR IGNORANCE AND NO TOLERANCE FOR THE IGNORANT.
LITTLE SYMPATHY FOR THEIR 'TROUBLED UPBRINGING', OR FOR THE IDIOTS THAT BROUGHT THEM INTO THIS WORLD.
ONLY IDIOTS COULD POSSIBLY PRODUCE NINE YEAR OLDS WITH CELL PHONES AND A DEFENSIVE NATURE THAT IS FIRST AND FOREMOST VIOLENT.

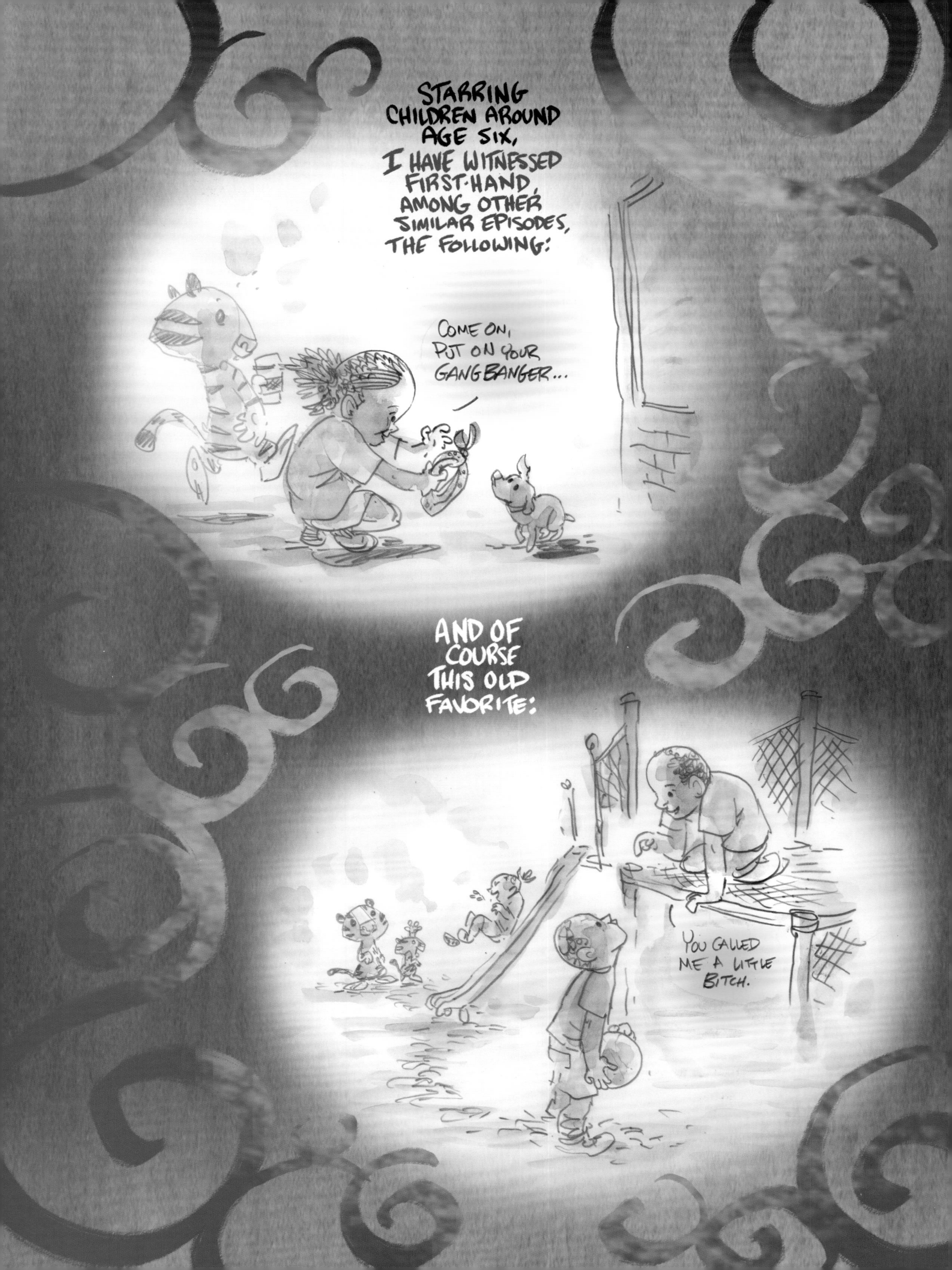
STARRING CHILDREN AROUND AGE SIX, I HAVE WITNESSED FIRST-HAND, AMONG OTHER SIMILAR EPISODES, THE FOLLOWING:
COME ON, PUT ON YOUR GANGBANGER...
AND OF COURSE THIS OLD FAVORITE:
YOU CALLED ME A LITTLE BITCH.

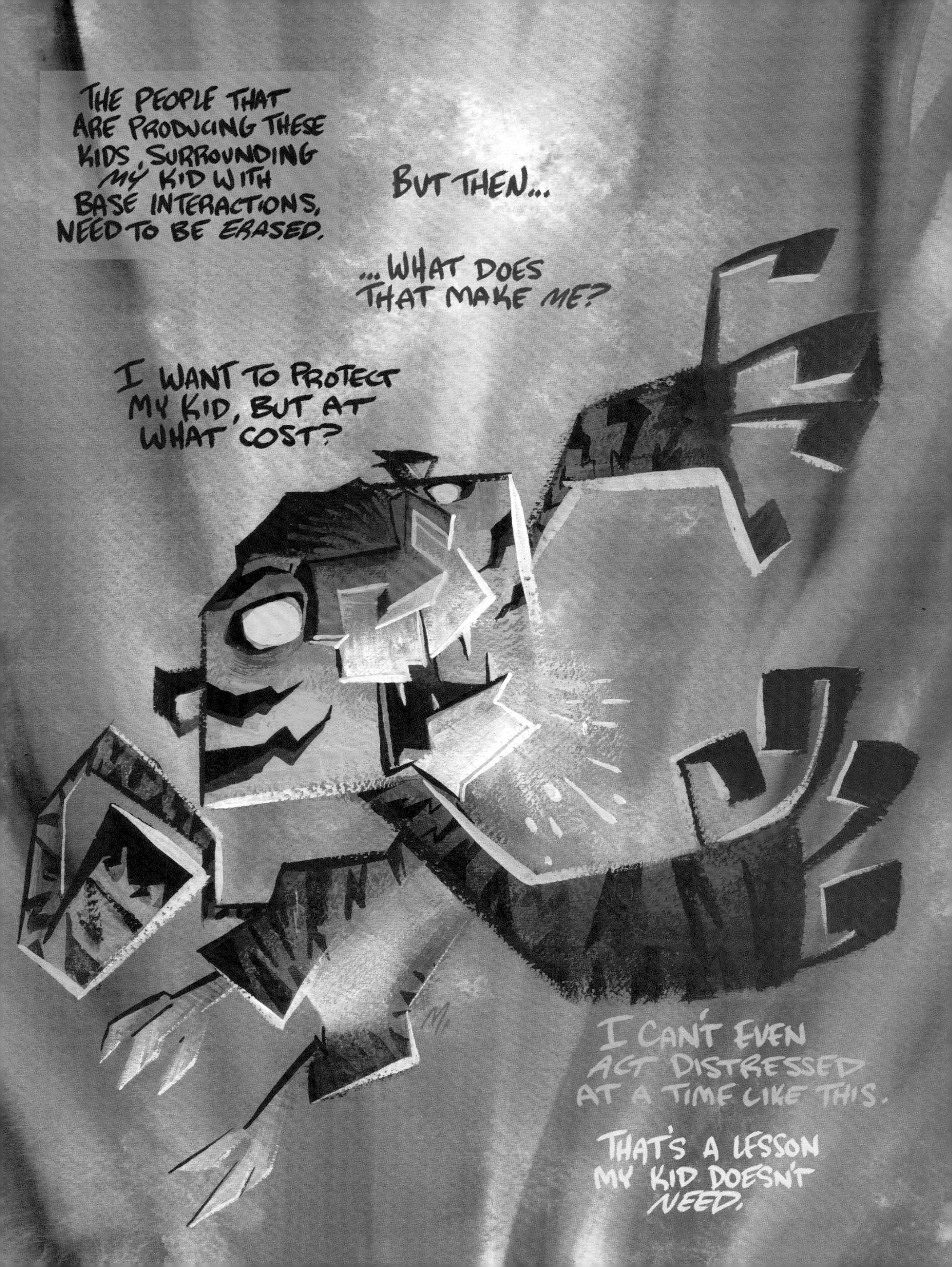
THE PEOPLE THAT ARE PRODUCING THESE KIDS, SURROUNDING MY KID WITH BASE INTERACTIONS, NEED TO BE ERASED.
BUT THEN...
...WHAT DOES THAT MAKE ME?
I WANT TO PROTECT MY KID, BUT AT WHAT COST?
I CAN'T EVEN ACT DISTRESSED AT A TIME LIKE THIS.
THAT'S A LESSON MY KID DOESN'T NEED.

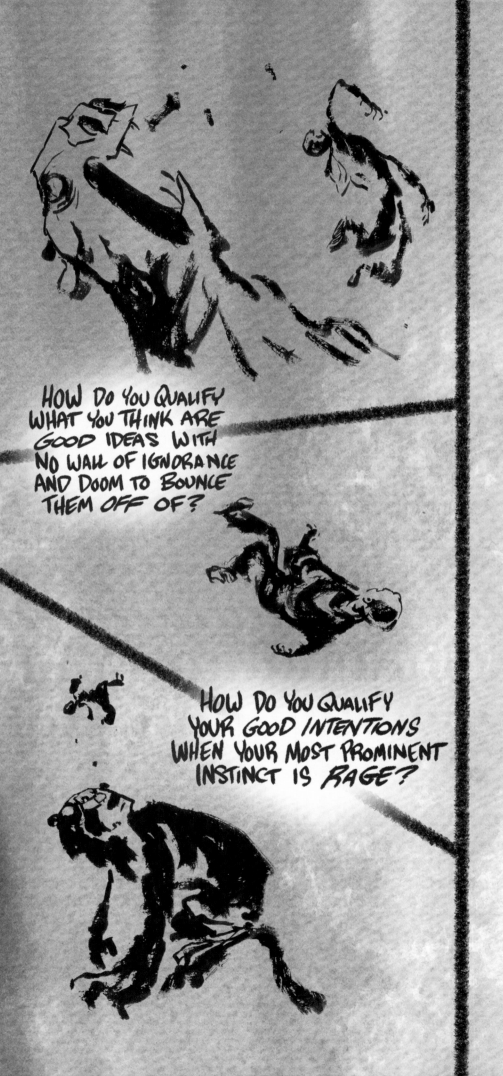

HOW DO YOU QUALIFY WHAT YOU THINK ARE GOOD IDEAS WITH NO WALL OF IGNORANCE AND DOOM TO BOUNCE THEM *OFF OF?*

HOW DO YOU QUALIFY YOUR GOOD INTENTIONS WHEN YOUR MOST PROMINENT INSTINCT IS *RAGE?*

WHEN THE BEST ANSWER SEEMS TO BE, IRONICALLY, THE MOST PARALLEL?

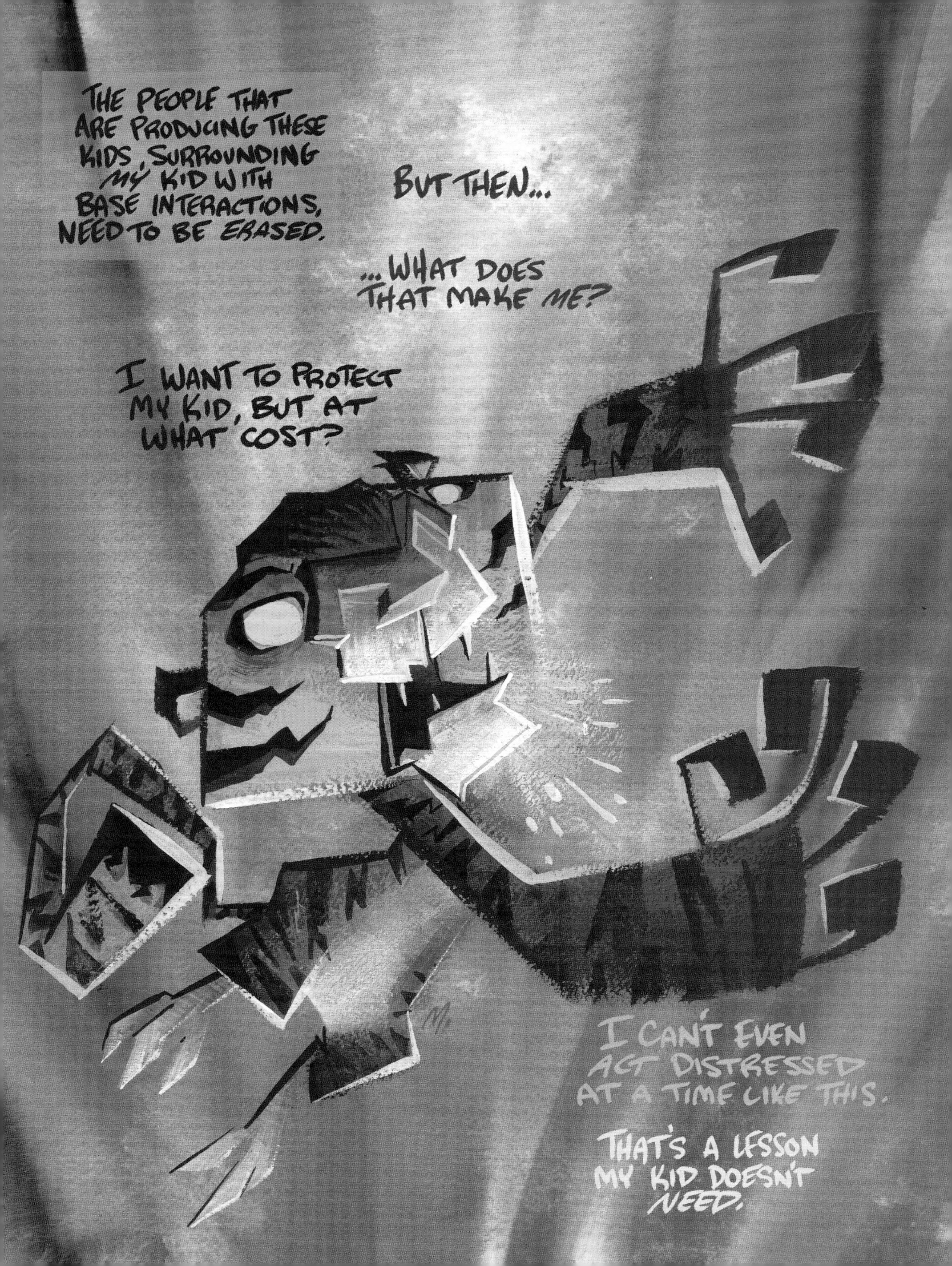

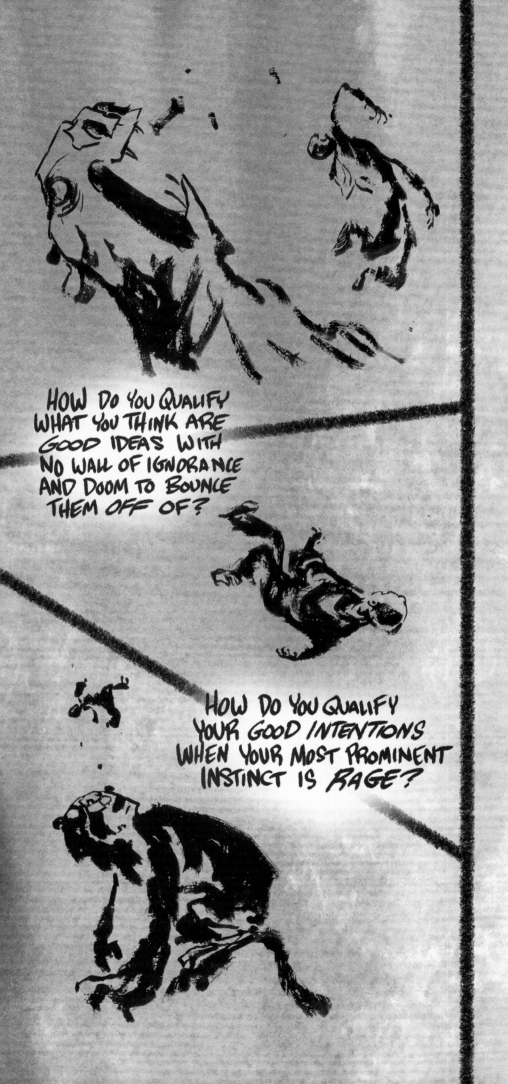

HOW DO YOU QUALIFY WHAT YOU THINK ARE GOOD IDEAS WITH NO WALL OF IGNORANCE AND DOOM TO BOUNCE THEM *OFF* OF?

HOW DO YOU QUALIFY YOUR *GOOD INTENTIONS* WHEN YOUR MOST PROMINENT INSTINCT IS *RAGE?*

WHEN THE BEST ANSWER SEEMS TO BE, IRONICALLY, THE MOST PARALLEL?

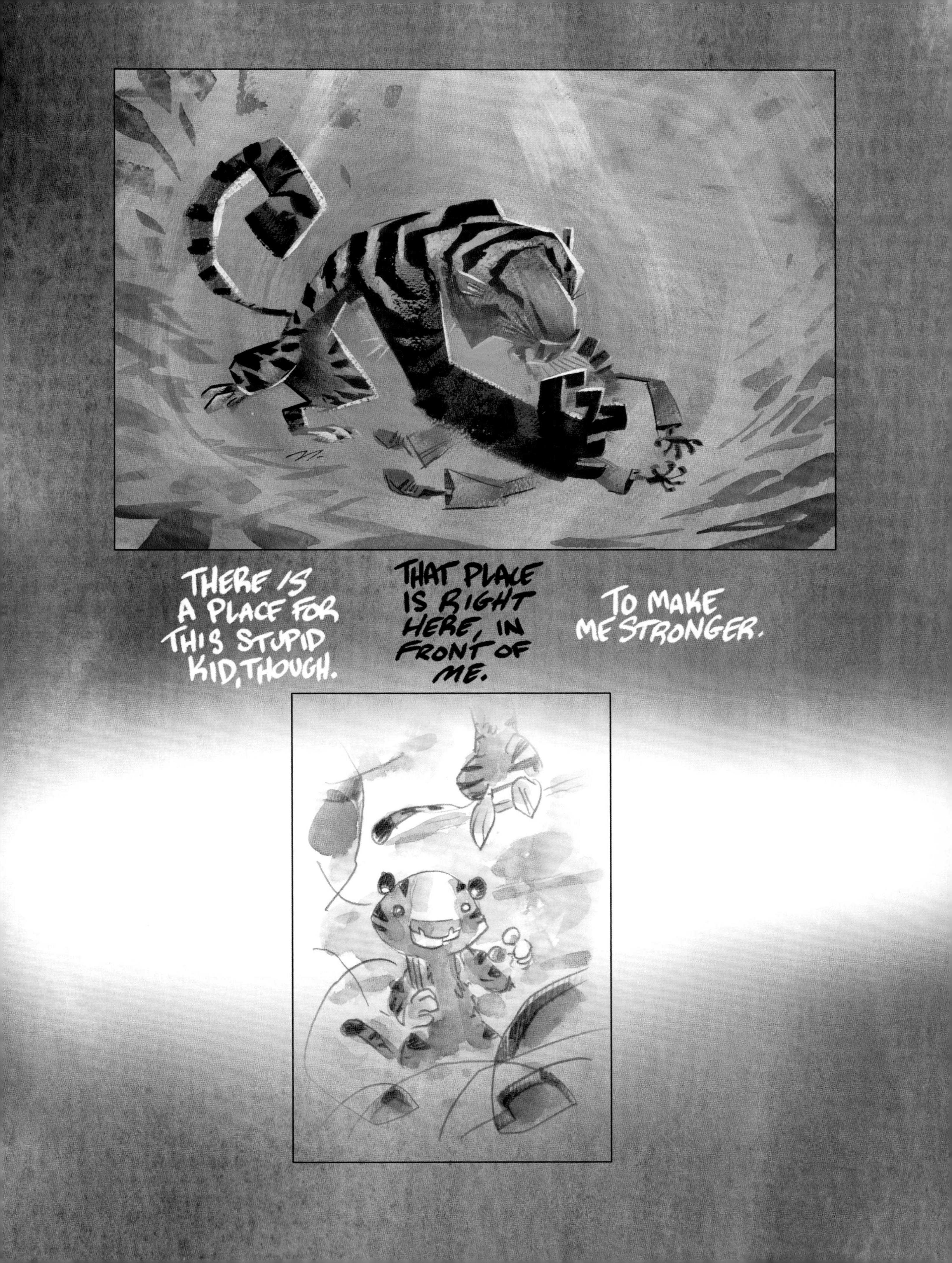
THERE IS A PLACE FOR THIS STUPID KID, THOUGH.
THAT PLACE IS RIGHT HERE, IN FRONT OF ME.
TO MAKE ME STRONGER.

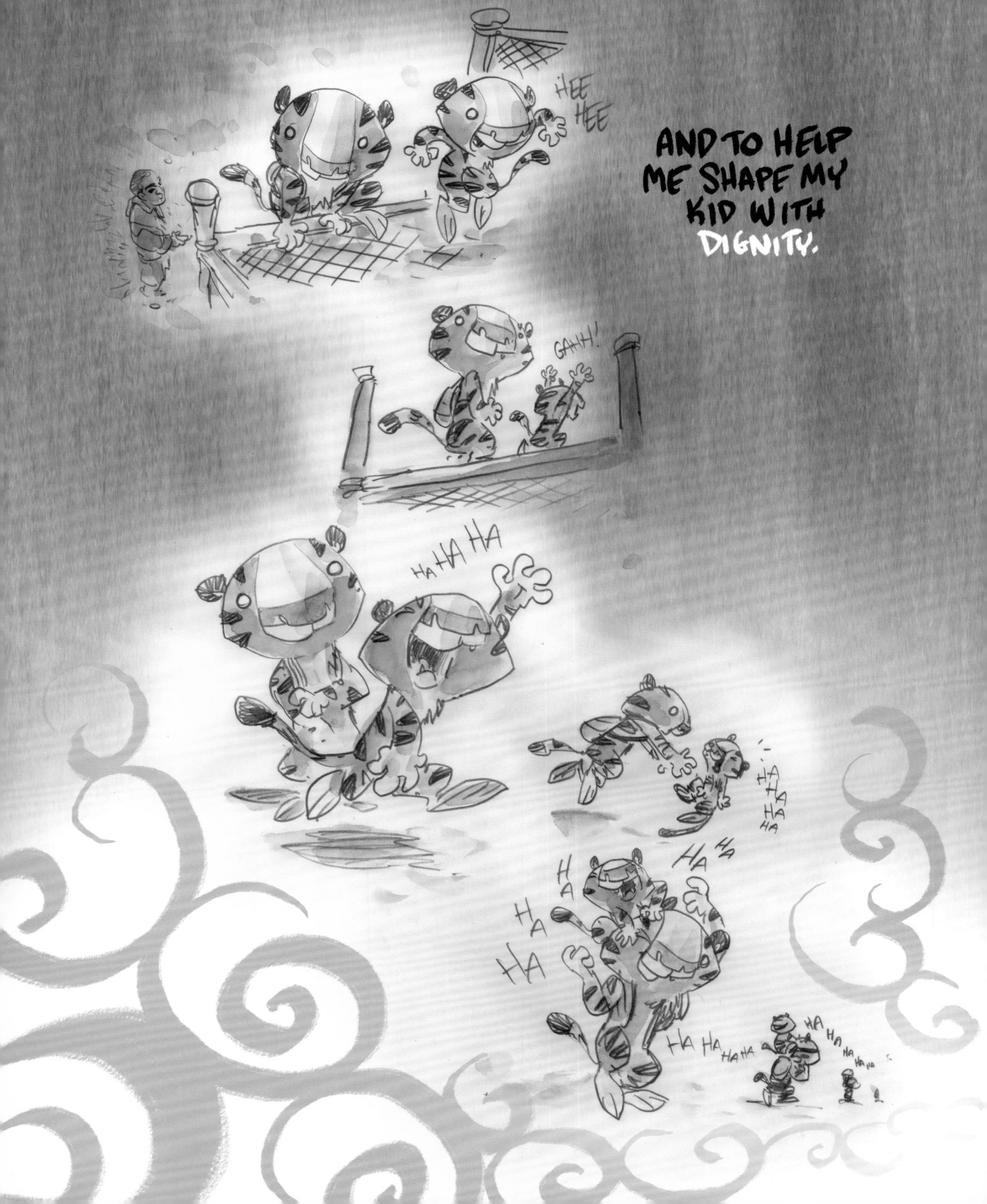
HEE HEE
AND TO HELP ME SHAPE MY KID WITH DIGNITY.
GAHH!
HA HA HA HA
HA HA HA HA
HA HA HA HA
HA HA HA HA HA
HA HA HA HA HA HA HA

YOU MAY HAVE NOTICED THAT *MENTALLY* I TEND TO DRIFT OFF. THEY LIKED TO CALL IT *DAYDREAMING*, BACK IN THE ERA OF *ROCKWELL* CALENDARS, WHEN *GEORGE BAILEY* THREATENED TRIPS TO THE FIJI ISLANDS AND TEENAGERS HOPPED UP THEIR DADS' OLD COUPES.

MY WIFE CALLS IT "BEING IN MY HEAD", WHICH IS ACTUALLY PRETTY CHARMING.

I WAS NEVER DIAGNOSED WITH ANY OFFICIAL ATTENTION DEFICIT DISORDERS OR ANYTHING, AND MY SON HASN'T BEEN, EITHER. BUT I CATCH HIM LEAVING INTO HIS HEAD, LIKE I DO.

I CAN SIT ALMOST ANYWHERE, ALONE, IN A GROUP, WHATEVER, AND SOME LITTLE THING WILL TAKE ME OUT.

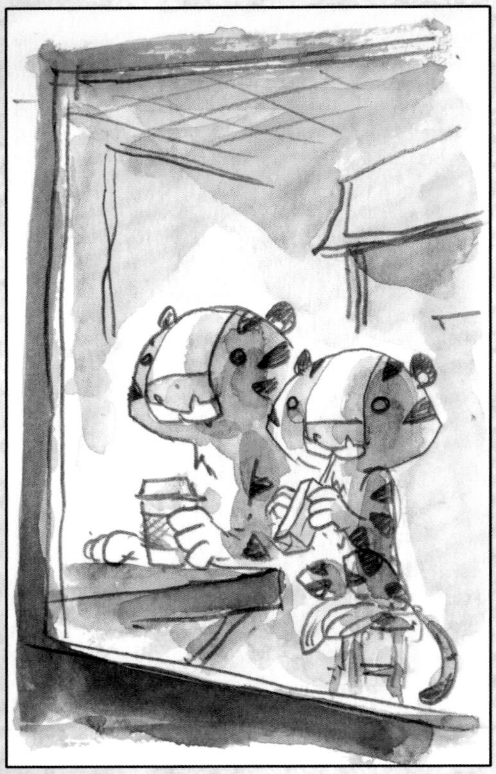

I STARE OUT PAST WHAT'S IN FRONT OF ME AND MY MIND *RACES*, NOT AMONGST JUMBLED THOUGHTS, REALLY, BUT IN A DRIVEN, UNIQUE PATH.

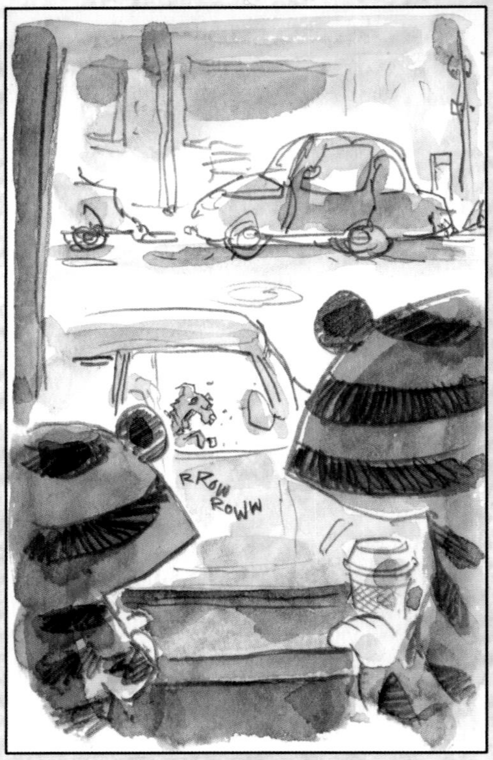
RROW ROWW

IT'S WHERE A LOT OF MY STORIES COME FROM. ODD BITS FIND THEMSELVES TRAVELLING THE SAME TRAIN OF THOUGHT ALL AT ONCE.

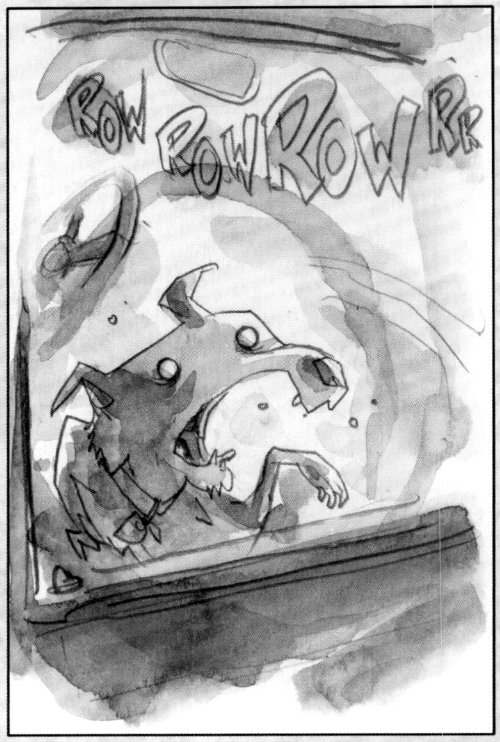
ROW ROWROWRRR

THEN, SOMETHING WILL PULL ME BACK.

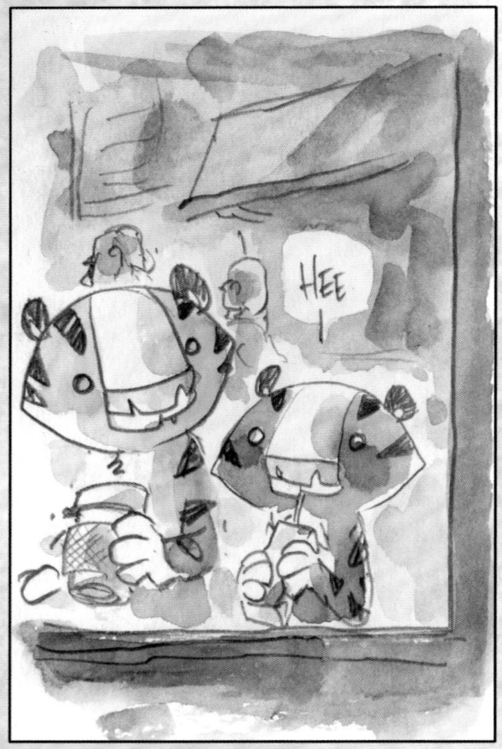
HEE

I HOPE HE'S FINDING THAT PLACE.

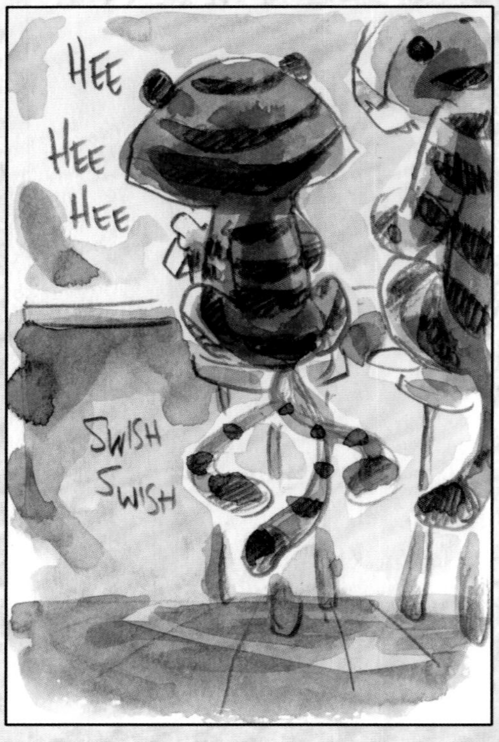
HEE
HEE
HEE
SWISH
SWISH

A PLACE LIKE THAT, FOR A KID, IT'S *MAGIC*.

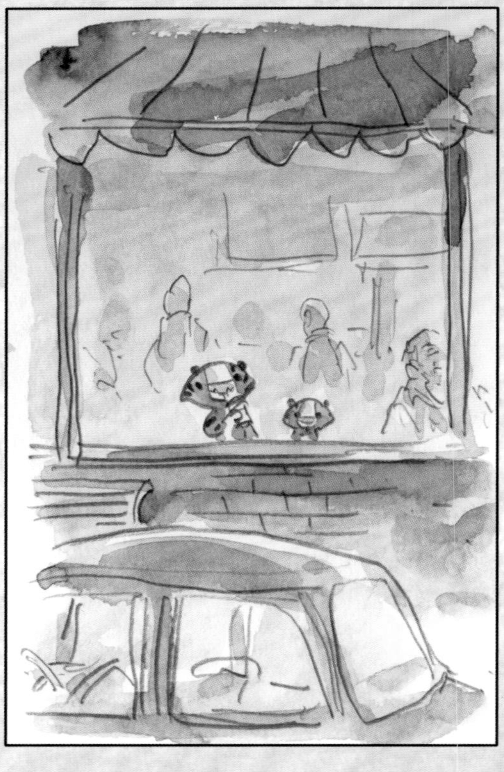

SOLVING *PROBLEMS*, MAKING *MUSIC*, BUILDING *WORLDS*.

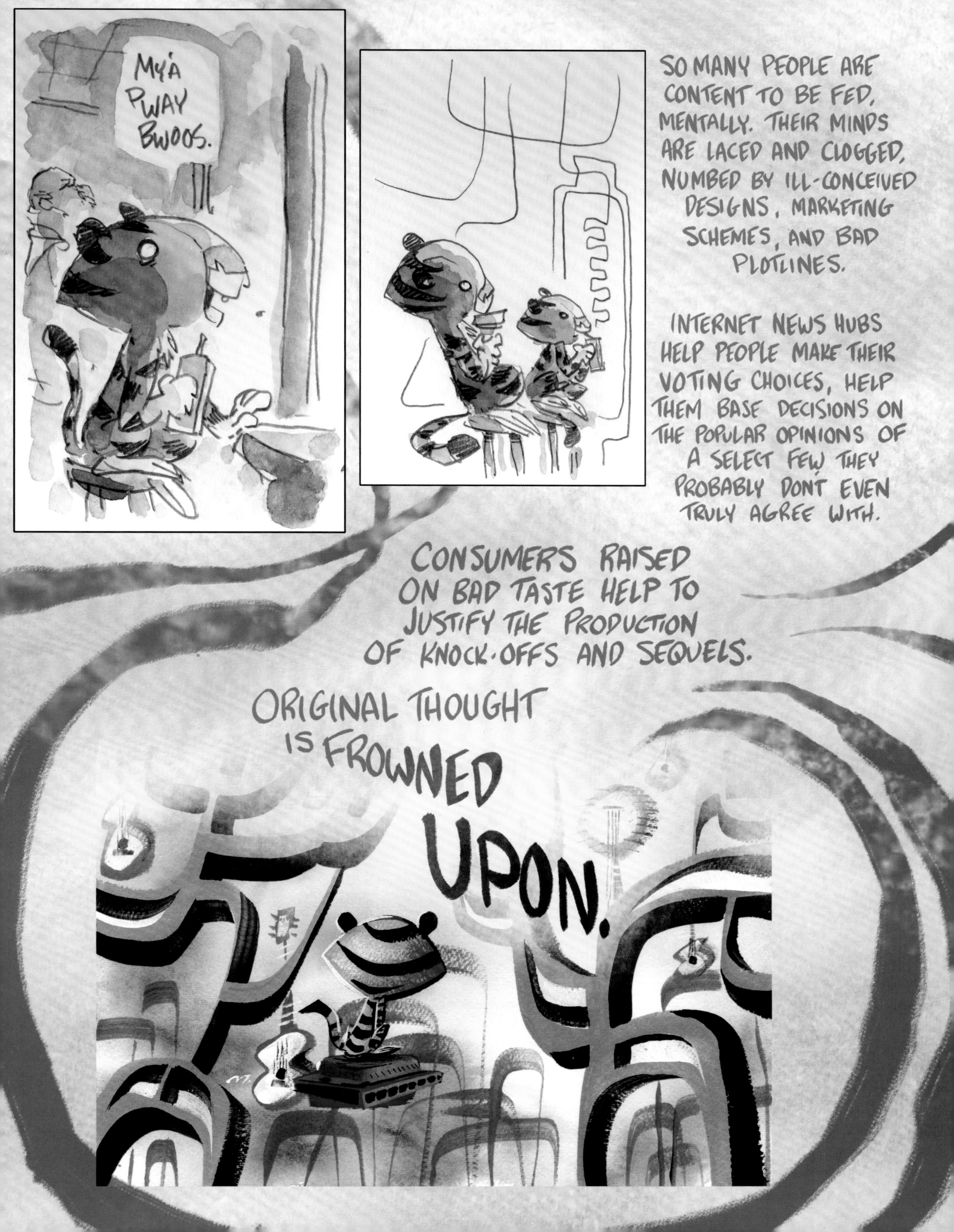
MY'A PWAY BWOOS.
SO MANY PEOPLE ARE CONTENT TO BE FED, MENTALLY. THEIR MINDS ARE LACED AND CLOGGED, NUMBED BY ILL-CONCEIVED DESIGNS, MARKETING SCHEMES, AND BAD PLOTLINES.
INTERNET NEWS HUBS HELP PEOPLE MAKE THEIR VOTING CHOICES, HELP THEM BASE DECISIONS ON THE POPULAR OPINIONS OF A SELECT FEW THEY PROBABLY DONT EVEN TRULY AGREE WITH.
CONSUMERS RAISED ON BAD TASTE HELP TO JUSTIFY THE PRODUCTION OF KNOCK-OFFS AND SEQUELS.
ORIGINAL THOUGHT IS FROWNED UPON.

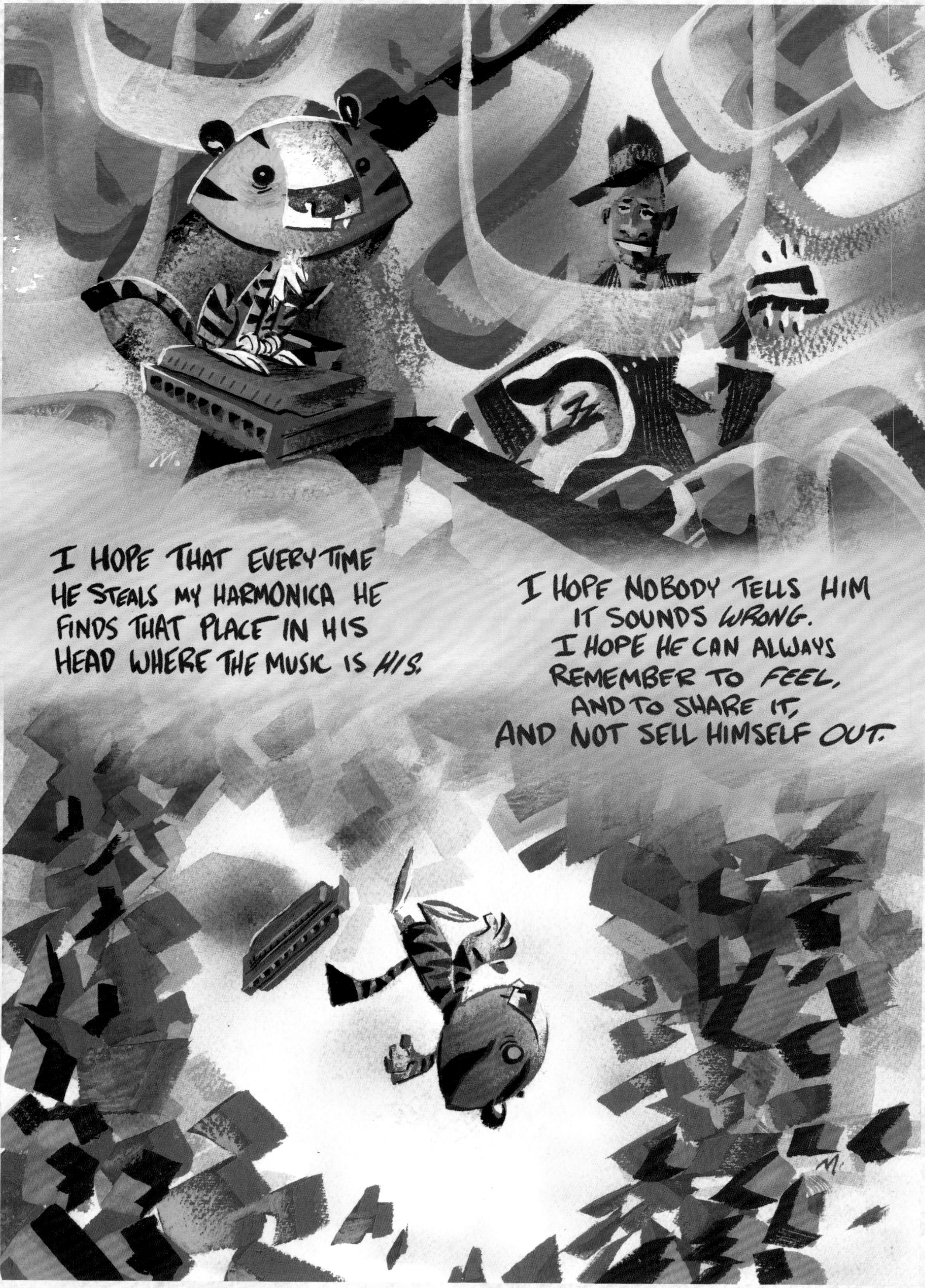
I HOPE THAT EVERY TIME HE STEALS MY HARMONICA HE FINDS THAT PLACE IN HIS HEAD WHERE THE MUSIC IS *HIS*.
I HOPE NOBODY TELLS HIM IT SOUNDS *WRONG*. I HOPE HE CAN ALWAYS REMEMBER TO *FEEL*, AND TO SHARE IT, AND NOT SELL HIMSELF *OUT*.

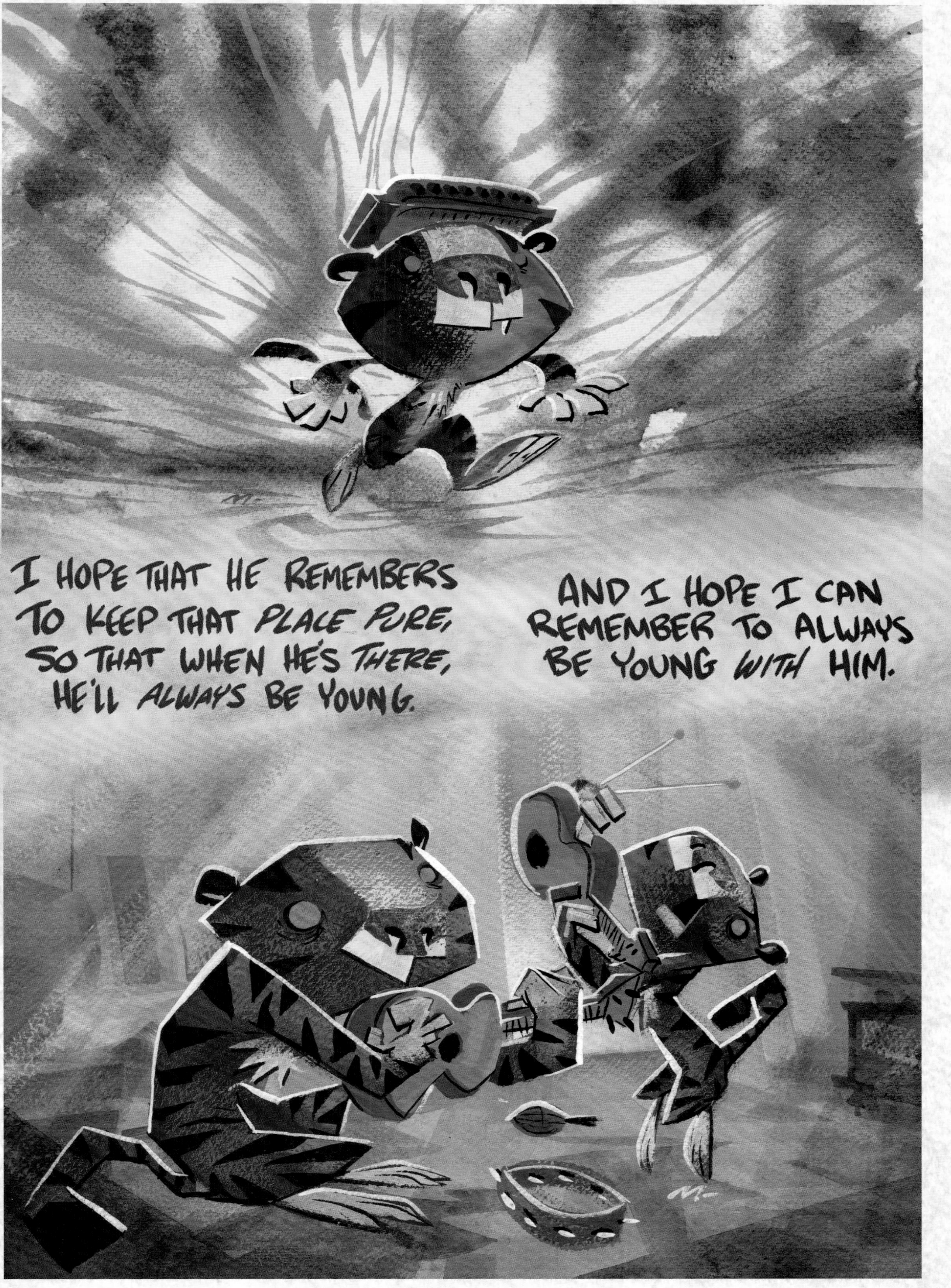

I HOPE THAT HE REMEMBERS TO KEEP THAT PLACE PURE, SO THAT WHEN HE'S THERE, HE'LL ALWAYS BE YOUNG.
AND I HOPE I CAN REMEMBER TO ALWAYS BE YOUNG WITH HIM.

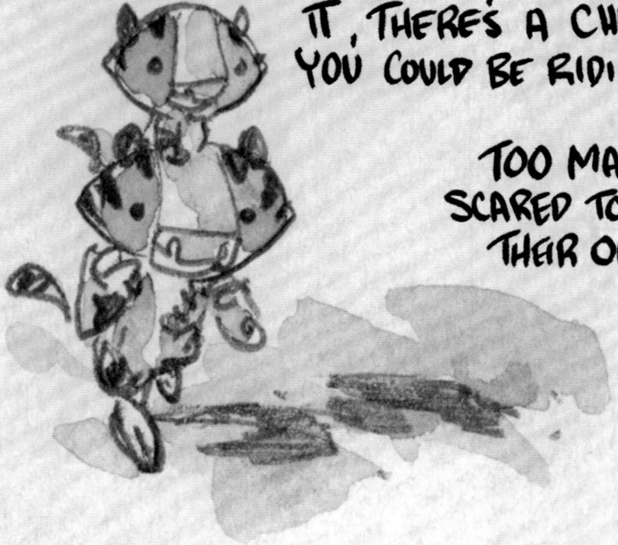

IF YOU HAVE AN IDEA, AND YOU *VOICE* IT, THERE'S A CHANCE YOU COULD BE RIDICULED.

TOO MANY PEOPLE ARE SCARED TO DISAPPEAR INTO THEIR OWN THOUGHTS.

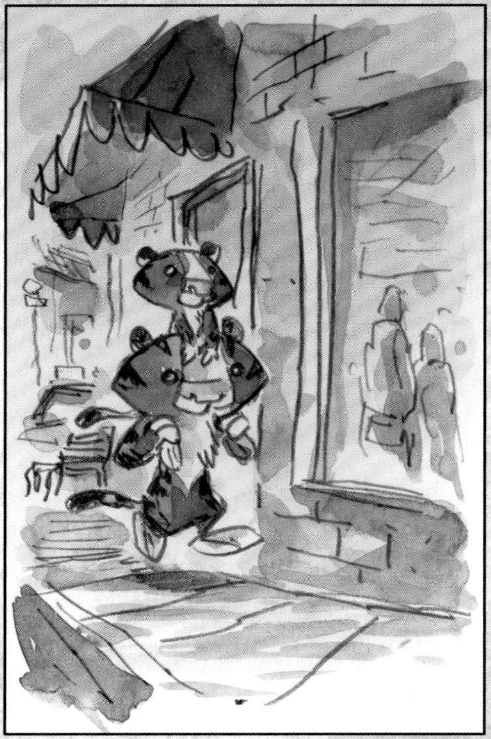

THERE'S A *FEAR* OF BEING RANKED AMONG THE IMMATURE, THE LAZY, AND EVEN THE *INSANE*.

BUT CONFIDENCE AND ORIGINALITY ARE *NURTURED* DURING THE EXPLORATIONS OF THE SOLITARY MIND.

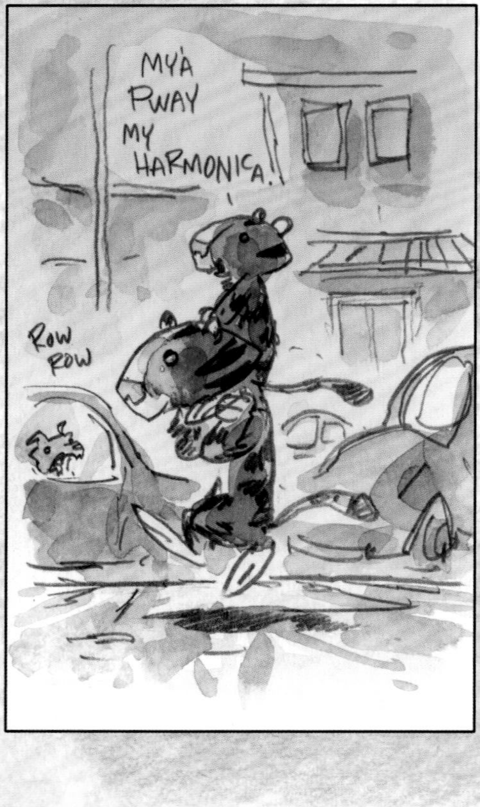
MY'A PWAY MY HARMONICA!
ROW ROW

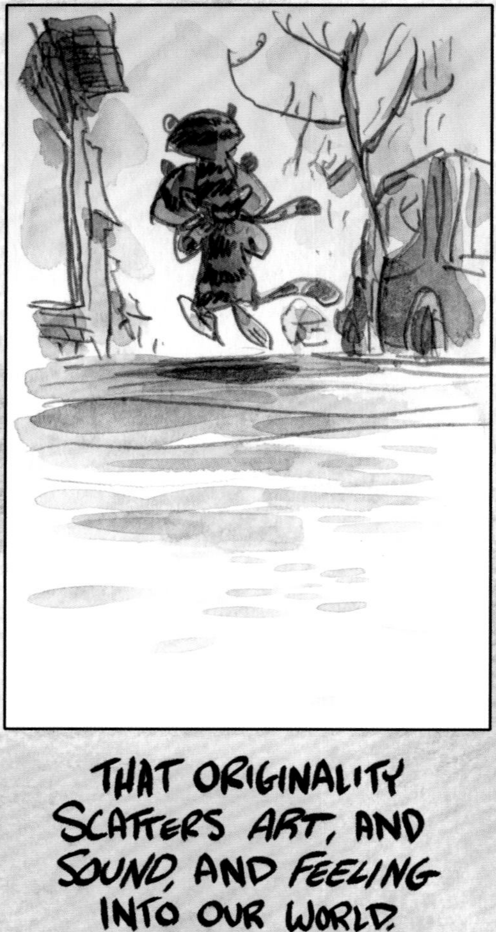

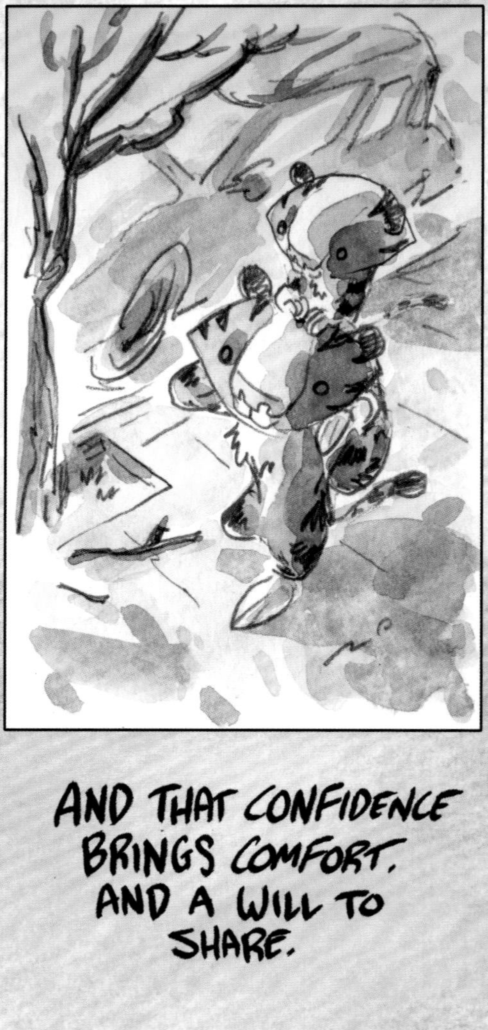

THAT ORIGINALITY SCATTERS *ART*, AND *SOUND*, AND *FEELING* INTO OUR WORLD.

AND THAT CONFIDENCE BRINGS *COMFORT*. AND A WILL TO SHARE.

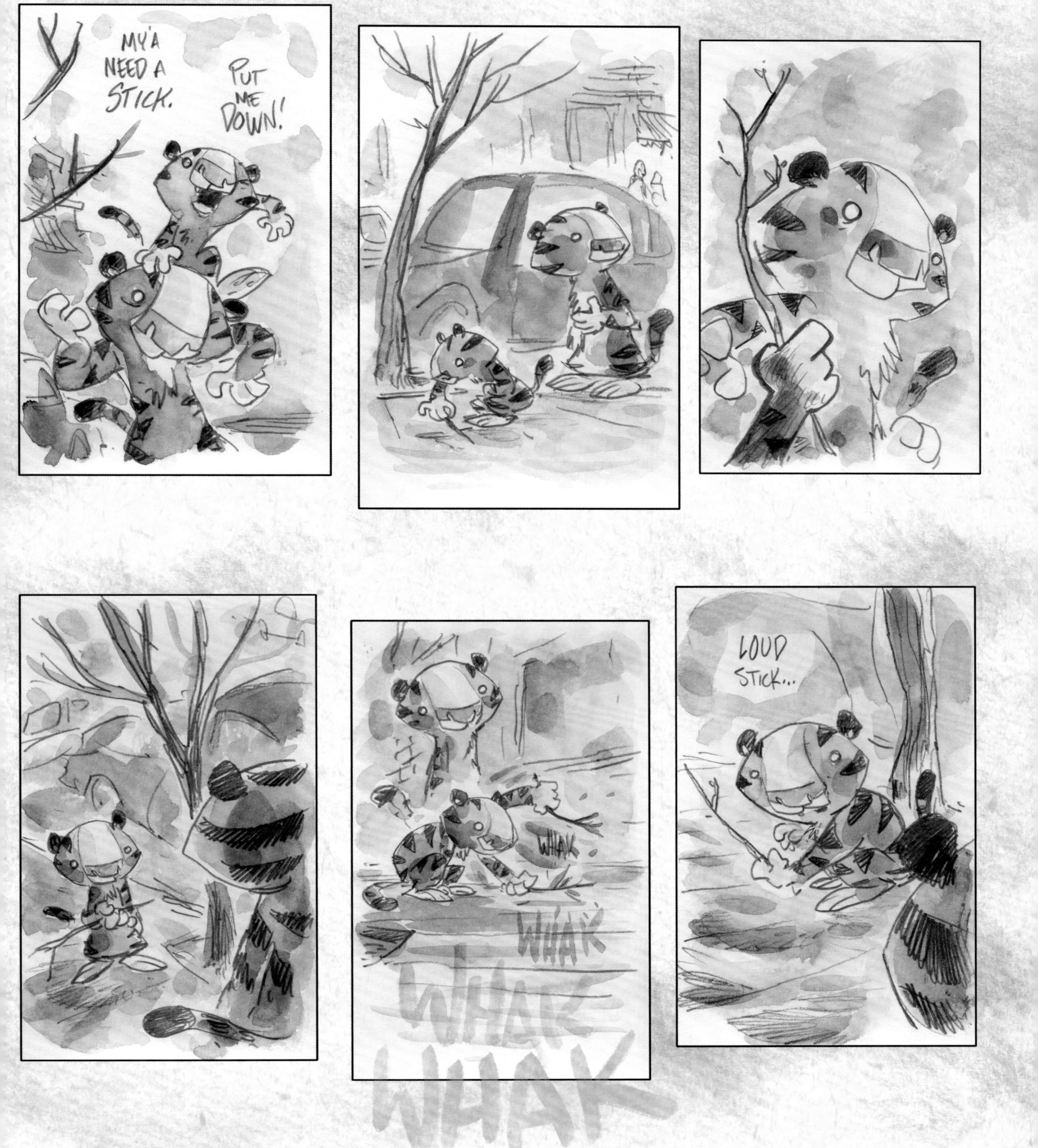
MY'A NEED A STICK.
PUT ME DOWN!
WHAK
WHAK
WHAK
WHAK
LOUD STICK...

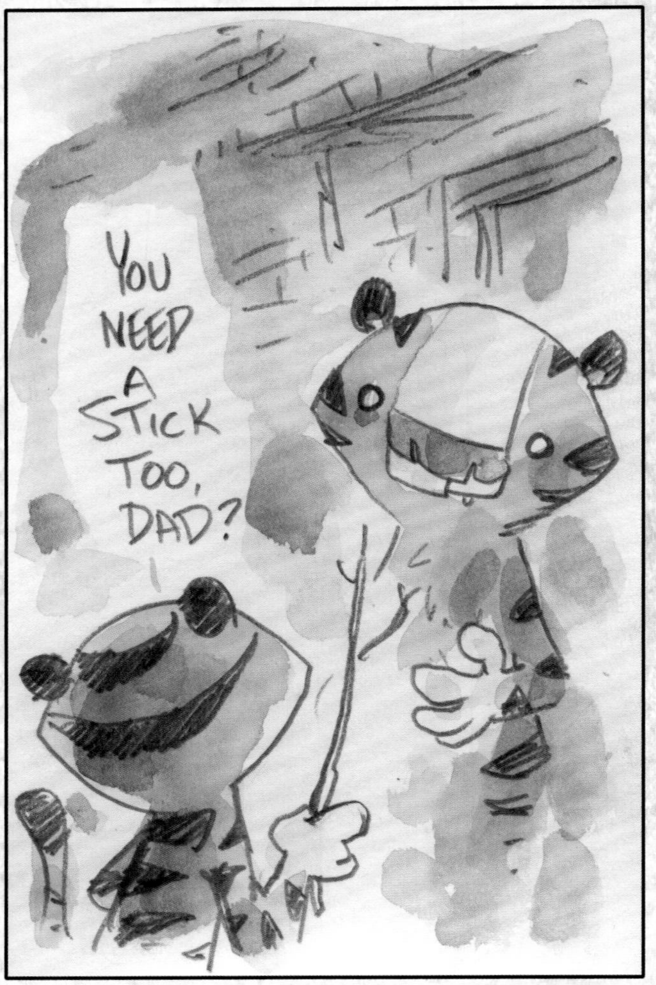
YOU NEED A STICK TOO, DAD?

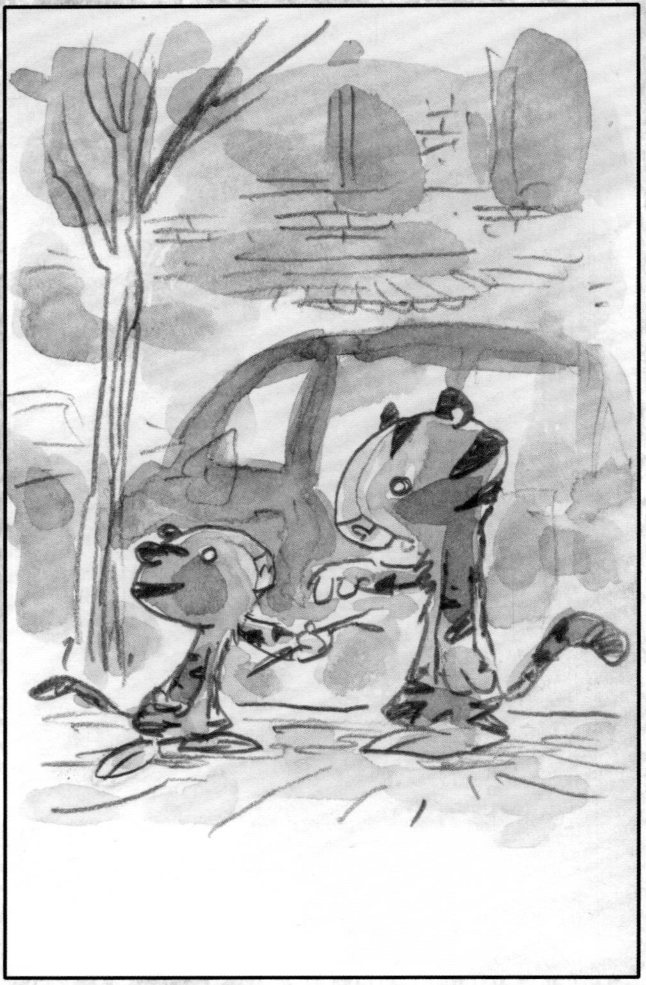

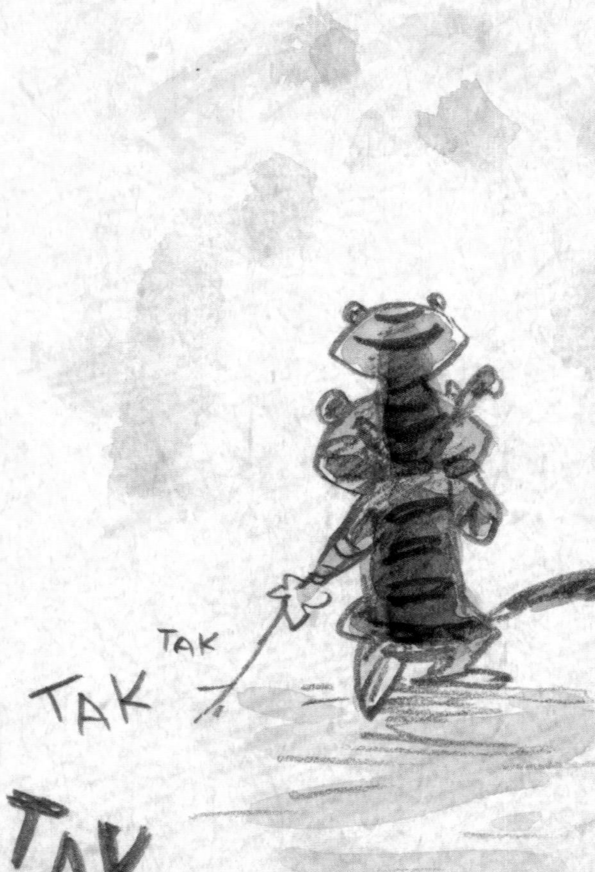
TAK
TAK
TAK

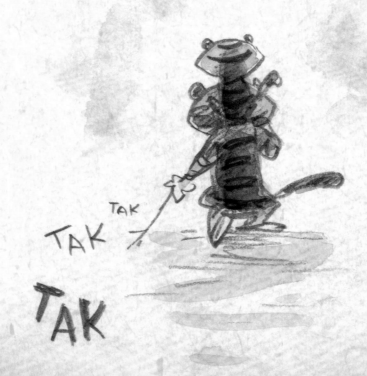